CW00549087

JONATHAN LEWIS and MIRAND/
Jonathan and Miranda have previous
award-winning play *Our Boys* (1995
Donmar Warehouse, London; *Lies With Short Legs*, as well as
a short film, *Beggar's Belief*.

JONATHAN LEWIS
Jonathan has directed much of his own theatre work, including:
Our Boys; *A Comedy of Arias* (2004) at the Pleasance, Edinburgh,
and the New Ambassadors Theatre, London; *The Pitch*, in
conjunction with advertising agency TBWA/London, at the
Soho Theatre, London. For television, he has written and directed
dramas for Granada, Carlton and the BBC and wrote, directed
and produced the short film, *Beggar's Belief*. Other directing
credits include David Williamson's *The Club*; *Breakfast With
Jonny Wilkinson* (2006) at the Menier Chocolate Factory; as
well as at the Bush Theatre and the Old Red Lion in London,
and the Northcott and Taliasan Theatres in Exeter and Swansea
respectively. Jonathan's awards include the Writers' Guild Award
for Best New Fringe Play and TAPS New Television Writer of
the Year; he was nominated for the Lloyd's Bank Playwright of
the Year Award. He most recently directed the Contemporary
Theatre Course at the E15 Drama School, London.

MIRANDA FOSTER
Miranda has worked extensively as an actress in the theatre,
most recently in the UK tour of *Festen* (2006) directed by
Rufus Norris, and on television in *The Trial of Gemma Lang*
(2007), written and directed by Jed Mercurio. She spent
several years at the National Theatre, playing leading roles in
both classical and new plays – working amongst others with
David Hare and Howard Brenton on the original production of
Pravda, with Richard Eyre and Dusty Hughes on *The Futurists*;
Sarah Daniels and John Burgess on *Neaptide*; Peter Hall and
Adrian Mitchell on *Animal Farm*; and with Peter Gill on *The
Women*; as well as many other projects at the National Theatre
Studio. She has also worked on new plays at the Bush, the
Young Vic, the Gate, the Lyric Hammersmith, the Orange Tree,
and Hampstead Theatre.

Jonathan Lewis

and

Miranda Foster

ALL MOUTH

NICK HERN BOOKS

London

www.nickhernbooks.co.uk

A Nick Hern Book

All Mouth first published in Great Britain as a paperback original
in 2007 by Nick Hern Books Limited, 14 Larden Road,
London W3 7ST

All Mouth copyright © 2007 Jonathan Lewis and Miranda Foster

Jonathan Lewis and Miranda Foster have asserted their right
to be identified as authors of this version

Cover image: Feast Creative
Cover design: Ned Hoste, 2H

Typeset by Country Setting, Kingsdown, Kent, CT14 8ES
Printed and bound in Great Britain by Biddles, King's Lynn

A CIP catalogue record for this book is available from
the British Library

ISBN 978 1 85459 593 5

All Mouth was first performed at the Menier Chocolate Factory, London, on 30 May 2007 (previews from 23 May), with the following cast:

DIGBY	Christopher Benjamin
MEL	Caroline Harker
PADDY	Simon Chandler
ROD	James Russell
GREG	Nigel Whitmey

Director   Jonathan Lewis
Designer   Anthony Lamble
Sound Design   Seb Frost
Lighting Design   Steve Barnett
Production Manager   Simon Sturgess
Set Construction   Bob Knight
Costume Supervisor   Shanti Freed
Company Stage Manager   Amanda Tait
Stage Manager   Kirk Woodley

For the Chocolate Factory:

General Manager   Tom Siracusa
Production Coordinator   Lucy McNally
Production Assistant   Jaqueline Kolek
Producer   David Babani

ALL MOUTH

Characters
in order of appearance

MEL, *early forties*

GREG, *late thirties*

DIGBY, *late sixties*

PADDY, *mid-fifties*

ROD, *early twenties*

The actors play all the other offstage voices.

A forward slash in the text (/) marks the point at which the next speaker interrupts.

This text went to press before the end of rehearsals and may differ slightly from the play as performed.

ACT ONE

One

Blackout.

MEL (*voice-over*). 'There's nothing I like better than excellent cleaning, and with new Green Ariel I'm really doing my bit for the environment.'

The lights come up on a sound studio in Soho. MEL is in front of a microphone and monitor with headphones. All the other people we only hear.

SOUND ENGINEER. OK Mel, the whole thing's on a seven with synch, but if you could squeeze me a second on the front –

VOICE 1. Hello, Melanie.

MEL. Hello.

VOICE 1. She's very 'up'.

MEL. So I can see.

VOICE 1. Modern woman. Does it all. The job, the kids. You know the type.

MEL. Uh-huh.

VOICE 1. Enjoys the challenge.

MEL. And what was wrong with the original voice?

VOICE 1. Sorry?

MEL. Looked like she was giving it plenty of 'up'.

VOICE 1. Oh, I see. Well, it's, er . . .

VOICE 2. Hello, Melanie. Nick, from the agency.

MEL. Hello, Nick.

VOICE 2. It was the timbre of her voice more than anything else.

MEL. Right.

VOICE 2. The timbre didn't quite work for us.

MEL. Why's that, then?

VOICE 2. It was too young.

MEL. She is young.

VOICE 2. Plus there was an 'up' thing. It wasn't the right sort of 'up'.

VOICE 1. Melanie, this is Gavin.

VOICE 2. Gavin's the client, Melanie.

VOICE 1. Essentially, Melanie, in a nutshell, the voice is too smug. Not aspirational enough. And we're looking for, er . . . sort of, er . . . cleaner, less murky, more flirty . . .

MEL. OK –

VOICE 1. We want that . . . 'hope-around-the-corner' feeling.

SOUND ENGINEER. OK then, Mel. Setting back. Bed'll be underneath. And on the green.

MEL. Right. 'Hope-around-the-corner', then.

Lights down on MEL.

The lights come up on a studio flat in Soho. There is a front door leading to a landing and staircase, a small kitchen area and a bathroom. Piles of lists and CDs, records, eight-tracks and even seventy-eights strewn everywhere, along with the remains of a takeaway, coffee cups and other detritus. A duvet is spread out on the sofa.

GREG *enters. He is on his mobile, hand over his other ear.*

GREG. So, is that a definite promise or a fuck-off promise, like *Casualty* was? Yup. Yup. All right. Sorry. I will. Yup, I'll try. I mean, how many times do they have to see me? Yeah, what? Sorry? I can't . . . Sorry, sorry. I know. I'm still in the frame. Yeah, I printed out the pages, and they liked the Irish? Bye. (*Hangs up.*) Fuck!

Lights down on GREG *and up on* MEL.

VOICE 1. What did we think?

VOICE 2. First one was nice.

VOICE 1. It was, wasn't it?

VOICE 2. Third one was nice too.

VOICE 1. Yes, it was.

VOICE 2. Nice as the first?

VOICE 1. I thought so.

VOICE 2. Maybe the second half of the first one and the first half of the third one?

VOICE 1. I liked take four. That was different altogether.

VOICE 2. Completely different.

VOICE 1. It had a need about it, didn't it?

VOICE 2. A nice need, though.

VOICE 1. Very nice.

VOICE 2. It was very different. Very . . .

MEL. Hopeful?

VOICE 1. Definitely more hopeful –

SOUND ENGINEER. And spot on with the synch and the timing.

VOICE 1. One more then, please.

SOUND ENGINEER. Why's that, then?

VOICE 1. I want one more.

VOICE 2. But we've got it.

VOICE 1 (*sharply*). Because we've booked for an hour.

SOUND ENGINEER. OK.

MEL. What would you like?

VOICE 1. Well . . . an alternative. You know. Mix it up a bit. Give us something even more interesting.

MEL. Right. 'Even more interesting', then.

Lights down on MEL *and up on* GREG.

SHARON (*on answerphone*). It's me, Digby. Monday's confirmed. You've got a Flash at eleven. Just radio at the moment. 'Big Box Groove'. Mr Sheen aren't happy, but I told them to fuck off. They were too tight to put you on sole usage, so what do they expect?

BELINDA (*on answerphone*). Message for Paddy. Darling, you're switched off. Can you get some Parma ham and olives –

SHARON (*on answerphone*). Me again, Digby. Dog biscuits. Two-thirty. 'Soho Sounds'. And the Coconut Zoo people want to go at three. I told them there might be an overrun and MDP said they'll wait for you as long as you don't bark or pee on them when you get there. Their joke not mine.

Lights down on GREG *and up on* MEL.

VOICE 2. Hello, Melanie. Nick again. As we are going for another one, do you think we could try it with more of a smile at the beginning?

MEL. Sorry? Big smile? Hint of a smile? Or just something a bit hysterical?

VOICE 2. We know she's going to find little Johnny's smelly football kit and she's going to be charmed. She's not going to be angry.

MEL. Christ, no.

VOICE 2. She's got a sense of humour.

MEL. Absolutely.

VOICE 2. It's important but it's fun. We're giving her an informed choice and she's going to choose.

VOICE 1. Fuck that! We need to want what she's got. And stress on the 'my' please. 'I'm really doing *my* bit for the environment.' So it's personal to her.

MEL. 'I'm really doing *my* bit for the environment.' OK.

VOICE 2. Are you sure? Shouldn't the stress be on 'bit'? 'I'm really doing my *bit* for the environment.'

VOICE 1. Rubbish. It's *her* bit that matters. *Her* bit.

VOICE 2. But then we lose the importance of the 'environmental contribution' bit.

VOICE 1. Oh, for fuck's sake.

MEL. Why don't I try one with more gravity on the 'excellent cleaning', so that she can earn the lighter pay-off with the 'I'm doing my bit', stressing them both. Then we see that it's important environmentally, but it's also fun.

VOICE 1. Yeah. That's, er . . . Yeah, that's basically what we're saying, yeah.

SOUND ENGINEER. Ready when you are then, Mel –

VOICE 1. And then if you could just throw it away at the end.

Blackout on the studio.

Two

MEL *enters the flat with a pint of milk and stops in her tracks, seeing the mess.*

MEL. Morning.

GREG. Eight records. That's all he's got to do. Choose eight records. He should be doing *In the Psychiatrist's Chair*. *Disco Inferno*!

GREG's mobile rings.

MEL. Don't be ridiculous.

GREG. *Disco Inferno*. Record number four.

MEL. Your phone!

GREG. Oh fuck, is it me?

> GREG *takes out his mobile, but he doesn't take the call.*

> Fucking gel people. Told Sharon I bullied Royce.

MEL. Royce at Sounds Right?

GREG. How could anyone bully Royce? No, it's not –

MEL. Are you sure –

GREG. Yes, I'm sure. It's got nothing to do with it.

MEL. Has Digby been in yet?

GREG. What?

MEL. Has Digby been in yet?

GREG. Don't know.

MEL. Why don't you just tell Sharon?

GREG. Are you joking? I'm not telling anyone.

MEL. I think you should.

GREG. Are you mad? Just before the strike?

MEL. Take her out. Confide in her –

GREG. She'd drop me like a stone. I'm broke, Mel.

MEL. She could get you phone-number jobs, bread-and-butter stuff.

GREG. I can't afford to strike.

MEL. You think I can?

GREG. Look, I'm seeing a specialist. OK?

MEL. Are you?

GREG. You promised –

MEL. I won't.

GREG. I wouldn't have –

MEL. I said I won't and I won't.

> GREG *moves an enormous pile of CDs away from the armchair.*

> Careful. That's part of the short-list area.

GREG. What?

MEL. Anything this side of the coffee table is now the short-list area.

GREG. Oh, for fuck's sake. 'It was at that point in my life, Kirsty, that I discovered – (*Reading the CD cover.*) 'I'm Every Woman', and what better way to wobble and sweat on those tropical nights than with my old friend Chaka Khan.'

MEL. He's not taking Chaka Khan.

GREG. What?

MEL. I said, he's not interested in Chaka Khan.

GREG. Do they still do *In the Psychiatrist's Chair*? And what's record number eight going to be? 'It's Raining Men'? Oh, this is disgusting.

> *The phone rings from the floor by the sofa and then mysteriously stops.*

MEL. It's not that bad.

GREG. No, I'm sorry, Mel, we all pussyfoot around him. He's a selfish old bugger. Who's he ponced all these off?

DIGBY (*from under the duvet*). Yes. Speaking. And what about the 78? I see. And lunch with Miss Young would be at what time? Thank you. Goodbye.

> DIGBY *gets up and goes into the bathroom.*

GREG. Oh God!

MEL. He's got a black eye.

GREG. What did I say?

MEL. How did he get a black eye?

GREG. Oh God.

MEL. He must have slept here last night. He must have been here all weekend.

GREG. Mel, do you think he heard me?

MEL. Of course he heard you.

GREG. What did I say?

MEL. You called him a selfish old bugger.

GREG. Shit –

MEL. And a ponce.

GREG. Bollocks.

MEL. You said he should be doing *In the Psychiatrist's Chair*.

GREG. Oh God. (*Whispers.*) Did I say anything about my ears?

> MEL *shakes her head.* DIGBY *comes out of the bathroom and puts his jacket on.*

MEL. Digby, are you all right?

DIGBY. Yes, I'm fine thank you.

MEL. Are you sure?

DIGBY. Yes, I'm fine. I slipped in the shower. Do excuse me, I have a session at eleven.

> DIGBY *leaves.*

Three

Later. Lights up on GREG *and* MEL *in the flat. Later,* PADDY *enters, speaking into his mobile phone.*

PADDY. Obviously that was a sight read. So if you did want to go ahead and we were in the studio we could really tighten it up and give it a good polish . . . Well, when you've been around the clock as many times as I have. Sorry? You googled me! I'm flattered. Really? Yes, it's Sharon Brauloff at Hudson's. Well, I hope so. It's a great script. Original *and* funny. A-I-G. That's right. Yes . . . The Anglo-Irish spelling, but everyone calls me –

GREG. Baldy –

PADDY. Baldy. Er, Paddy. Paddy Cummings –

GREG. That's my Paddy. Paddy Cummings-and-goings –

PADDY. Sorry?

GREG. Are you arranging a test?

PADDY. Well, er, yes, technically I could yes. Next, er . . . Why don't I ring you back?

GREG. He's arranging a test for next week! Do they know about the strike, Pad? They should all know about the strike that starts next week!

PADDY. Gosh, that's my next session, I'm afraid I'm going to have to –

GREG. NO TELLIES, NO INTERNET, NOTHING –

PADDY (*to* GREG). Will you – ?

GREG. Scab!

PADDY (*into the mobile*). OK. Yup. Yup. OK. Bye. Yup. Bye –

GREG. Scab! Scab! Scab!

PADDY (*flips the lid closed on his mobile*) Do you mind? That could be at least a term's school fees. I'll slip it in before.

GREG. Oh yeah!

MEL. Paddy, you're not going to break the strike . . .

PADDY. I'm not breaking the strike. We are not technically on strike until next week.

GREG. It's a great script. Original and funny. Can I suck your cock as well, sir?

PADDY. D'you know, some of us have it and some of us are –

GREG / PADDY. Just full of it.

PADDY. Wrong sex, by the way. Ludmilla's a producer at
Templemann's. Sounds very sexy, actually. Never wears
underwear, according to Gunter, but he says she's a bit
whiffy downstairs.

MEL. Ooh. Morning, Paddy.

PADDY. Morning, Melanie. How are you this morning?

MEL. Oh, loving life and feeling beautiful.

PADDY. Looking beautiful too, unlike this . . . this tenement
slum that is now passing for HQ. Morning, Gregory.

GREG. Morning, Baldy.

PADDY. Now then, Gregory. Any news?

GREG. I don't want to talk about it.

Silence.

They want to see me *again.*

PADDY. Again?

GREG. Tape all the siege scenes.

PADDY. Great. So you're still in the frame?

GREG. I just thought . . .

PADDY. Well, you see, there's so many of the bastards
involved in the decision-making process these days.
Especially for a 'regular'.

MEL. They're probably doing some market research.

PADDY. Seeing how popular he'd be with the housewives of
Norwich.

MEL. Still, let's be positive.

PADDY. Yup. Always best to be positive.

GREG. I just want to know. One way or the other. So I can get
on with my life.

PADDY. Yes, it's just a soap, love. It's not Hollywood, is it? If you get it, fine. If you don't, it's no big deal.

GREG. What do you mean?

PADDY. It's no big deal –

GREG. How can you say that?

PADDY. It's just a soap, Coco –

GREG. It's the most watched programme in Britain.

PADDY. I think that's being a bit generous, old fruit.

GREG. I don't think you quite understand what a life-changing event this could be. This isn't just a couple of episodes. This would be a year. A year on *EastEnders*. Just think about that.

PADDY *grimaces*.

I am this close to being the Reverend Michael Brennan.

MEL. Maybe it's because they want the real thing.

GREG. What – ?

MEL. Maybe that's why there's all this deliberation –

GREG. What are you talking about?

MEL. Well, they all want the real thing these days, don't they?

GREG. They want a real vicar – ?

MEL. Well, vicar-turned-actor.

GREG. What – ?

MEL. Or at least born again –

GREG. That's ridiculous.

PADDY. Absolutely.

GREG. D'you think?

MEL. Could be.

PADDY. How well do you know your Bible?

GREG. Christ Almighty!

MEL. Now you're talking.

Blackout.

Four

In the blackout we hear the beginning of TOM's *answerphone message. During the message, the lights come up on the flat.* MEL *and* PADDY *are sitting on the sofa.*

TOM (*on answerphone*). Mel, why are you pulling this joint-care-and-control crap now? I thought we agreed. What's the point of uprooting the kids every other week? We've already been through that. This is their home. You can have as much contact with them as you want –

MEL. But I can't!

TOM (*on answerphone*). Do you really want to put the kids through any more of this?

MEL. I didn't see them at all this weekend because he forgot it was the 'Center Parcs treat'.

PADDY. Oh dear.

MEL. There's another woman living in my house. My children are being brought up by another woman. She's a fucking fitness instructor!

PADDY. It's appalling.

MEL. Who books weekend treats at Center Parcs. I don't want her bringing up my children.

PADDY. Absolutely.

MEL. I should never have left. Anything could happen. What if she decides she wants them to move?

PADDY. Quite.

MEL. I wanted to be the one at home.

PADDY. Is he still trying to paint?

MEL. Oh yeah. He's got a studio full of paintings. It's a wonderful studio. Cost me a fortune.

PADDY. Lord.

MEL. When I took Lily out for lunch she said she wouldn't have the garlic bread because she didn't want to be greedy. It's her favourite thing. She's seven, for God's sake. That's the fucking fitness instructor. No white wine for her in the evening. With her tight little cropped tops.

PADDY. That's not good.

MEL. What about you? Your older two. You still don't see much of them, do you?

PADDY. No. I'm still hoping . . . You know, one day, when they're older –

GREG enters, holding some pages from the EastEnders *script, a takeaway coffee, and a new Bible.*

GREG. Do you know how difficult it is trying to buy a Bible in this Godforsaken capital city of the world?

The front door buzzer sounds and MEL *presses the button on the entryphone.*

PADDY. By the by, there are a couple of new releases that Gunter would like us to have a look at and I was wondering, as the strike'll soon be upon us, you and Father Abraham might be able to squeeze me a diaristic window.

MEL. Oh God, all right then –

PADDY. As we'll all be sitting on our vocal chords, etcetera.

GREG's mobile gives a text alert. There's a knock at the door and MEL *opens it.* ROD *enters. He has a package in his hand.*

ROD. Hi.

MEL. Hello.

ROD (*to* PADDY *and* GREG). Hey.

MEL (*taking the package from* ROD). Where do I sign?

ROD. That's OK. It's for Digby Scott. Is he around?

He takes the package back.

MEL. It's Flat 2. We all sign for each other.

ROD. That's cool. I'll wait.

MEL. We all use this place. It'll be perfectly safe.

ROD. I'm, er . . . from the BBC.

PADDY. You're what?

ROD. Digby Scott. He's recording his *Desert Island Discs* –

PADDY. You're from the BBC?

GREG. Quickly, Paddy, where's your CV?

PADDY. Shut up. You're from the BBC?

MEL. Calm down, Paddy. He's not offering you a job.

ROD. We did a radio series together a couple of weeks ago. *At* the BBC. We got talking about music and shit, and there were a few tracks I said I'd burn for him.

PADDY. You're not a courier, then?

ROD. No. Well, yeah, I am. But I'm not at this moment here as a courier. Digby and I did the radio series together. *In Lieu of Love*?

MEL. I think you must be Rod.

ROD. That's right.

PADDY. Sorry? This is who?

MEL. Paddy, this is Rod . . .

Not a flicker from PADDY.

Rod.

PADDY. Oh! This is Rod, is it? Blimey.

MEL. Hello, Rod. We've heard a lot about you.

ROD. Have you?

MEL. Oh, yes.

The phone rings again loudly, but only once, and goes
straight to answerphone. GREG *is looking at his script.*

SHARON (*on answerphone*). This afternoon at three, Digby.
Test for something called 'Gonnadoo'. E-mailing script
now. Ring me to confirm. Thank you.

MEL *writes 'Gonnadoo, 3 p.m., Digby' on the whiteboard.*

ROD. Busy, then?

GREG. Always busy.

PADDY. Not at the moment, actually. Winding down.

GREG. Because of the strike.

ROD. What strike?

GREG. What do you mean, 'What strike'? The strike. Next
week. You must know about the strike. (*Beat.*) Well, that
bodes well –

ROD. Oh yeah, Digby mentioned the strike.

MEL. To stop the industry using synthetically-created voices.

GREG. They've been sampling our voices for years without us
knowing. Since the last strike, in fact –

MEL. You know, when someone texts your landline and you
get that computerised voice saying the message like a
robot? Well, now they've got the technology to make it
sound real.

GREG. So you can see where that's going, can't you?

MEL. We'd all be out of a job. Seriously, it'd put so many
people out of work. Not just us.

GREG. Do you know, they've been farming digitally-created
voices on massive hard drives.

PADDY. How can you farm voices on a hard drive?

GREG. No no no. In ten years they won't need any of us at all.

PADDY. Rubbish! It'll never catch on. They'll never be able to get any of the nuances. The humour, the irony –

GREG. We're fucked! We're all fucked!

MEL. Would you like a coffee?

ROD. Awesome.

MEL. Coffees all round then, Paddy.

PADDY. What? Right. Sorry, am I buying these, or do you want me to do home-made?

MEL. Whatever you feel your talents will stretch to.

PADDY. Right. It's just that I'm a bit brassically challenged if we're all going Americano.

ROD. So how many voice-overs do you do on an average week, then?

GREG. What?

ROD. How many do you do on an average week?

GREG. There is no average.

MEL. Have you done much yet, Rod? Digby said you'd just finished college.

ROD. Four lines on a telly and the radio series.

MEL. It's a start.

GREG. I bet they were four very good lines.

MEL. What about theatre?

ROD. Digby very kindly said he'd have a word with a contact at the National.

GREG. The National! Did he?

ROD. Yeah.

PADDY. He'd need a ouija board for that, old fruit. Milk and sugar?

ROD. One please. Black. I thought you top voice-over people kept off the dairy.

GREG. What?

MEL. Really?

ROD. Thanks. Yeah, that's what I read. Otherwise you get mucus and all that. You know – phlegm.

GREG. Sorry?

ROD. Phlegm.

PADDY. Charming.

ROD. That isn't true, then?

PADDY. I'm sure it is.

MEL. Just goes to show we're obviously not top voice-over turns.

There is a sound of a bike crashing to the floor in the corridor.

DIGBY (*off*). Christ Almighty! Who put this bloody bike here? Ow.

DIGBY *enters, limping and carrying a wad of fliers, stickers and strike paraphernalia – stuff to make banners and placards. He has a black eye.*

DIGBY. Christ, my foot! Just look what you've done to my – Ah, hello. It's you –

ROD. I'm so sorry, I thought there was enough room to squeeze by. I didn't want to get it nicked –

DIGBY. No, no. Absolutely. You leave it there –

ROD. Let me take a look at your foot. I'm a trained masseur, remember?

DIGBY. Are you – ?

PADDY. My God, Digby! What happened to your eye?

DIGBY. What? Oh . . . It was an accident. I . . . slipped in the shower.

PADDY. You slipped? What, the shower here? That's terrible. When did that happen?

DIGBY *sits.* ROD *helps him ease off his shoe.*

DIGBY. I see you've already met the gang.

ROD. Yeah.

PADDY. How the hell did you slip? I've never slipped. (*To* MEL.) Have you ever slipped in that shower?

DIGBY. Christ! Will you shut up? I just slipped. Now this is Rod, everyone. He played my son –

ROD. Derek –

DIGBY. Derek. That's right. Wonderful performance. In that radio series I did for the Beeb. You remember I said there was a boy who stood out? Well, this is he. And that's Melanie, that's Greg, and the trainspotter over there is Paddy.

ROD. Hi.

PADDY. Well, I think we'll have to invest in a non-slip mat!

GREG. What's all this?

DIGBY. I just bumped into Pig Jones and he asked whether we could construct these.

GREG. 'No pay, no say'?

DIGBY. There's all the kit for twenty banners. I've also put us down for shifts on the picket line.

MEL. What picket line?

PADDY. You did what?

GREG. 'Keep it real' –

DIGBY. Pig's already told me they're going to try and get all sorts of wankers in to break the strike, so we've got to make sure they all know they'll be on a union blacklist if they do. It'll give that ad mob one hell of a shock, I can tell you.

MEL. What, to see a bunch of actors standing outside a studio?

GREG. 'What do we want?' How was that? Can I go again?

DIGBY. It's tremendous publicity value. Imagine seeing Dodger and Pig Jones on a picket line. Pound to a penny that's going to make the news.

PADDY. Umm. 'Millionaire and Oscar-winner in bid to be' . . . what?

MEL. Taken seriously? Digby, we're not firemen. We'll be laughed at.

DIGBY. No we won't. Pig's absolutely hell-bent on this. We all are.

MEL. No one's going to take picketing actors seriously.

DIGBY. Course they are. When they know what we're fighting for. You won't get actors walking across a picket line.

GREG. No, more like running –

DIGBY. It'll be far too intimidating. We'll wear donkey jackets. Really look the part. What do you think, Rod? Show these wankers what for.

ROD. Whatever it takes.

GREG. Here we go! We're on the fucking waterfront!

DIGBY. God knows we've tried to be reasonable. But these internet bastards can't get away with it.

GREG. Course they can. They don't need us. We're fucked.

DIGBY. We are not fucked! 'We few, we happy few – '

GREG. Will be even fewer –

DIGBY. Christ! This is too important. Please. This isn't about us. It's about the future. We're drawing a line in the sand. Because, if we don't do it now there's going to be nothing left. For these kids. You mark my words, there'll be computerised people on the screen. Robot movie stars. There won't be any of us left. I will not stand by and let those bastards destroy this business. (*To* ROD.) Ooh, that's wonderful. It's an old theatre injury. Steep rake and cobblestones for a year. The designer's still winning fucking awards!

ROD (*to* PADDY). Can I just say, I saw you in a play when I was at school.

PADDY. Pardon?

ROD. At Stratford on a school trip. That's what threw me when I first came in. You were Hotspur in *Henry IV Part One*.

PADDY. Blimey! Was I? You've got a memory and a half.

ROD. I'll never forget it.

DIGBY. Everyone else did.

PADDY. Ah yes. 'My liege, I did deny no prisoners'. I did it Northumberland.

DIGBY. Really? We were wondering . . .

PADDY.
   'But when the blast of war blows in our ears,
   Then imitate the action of the tiger.'

DIGBY. Rubbish.

PADDY. What?

DIGBY. You're mixing your histories.

PADDY. No I'm not.

DIGBY. Do excuse us. You're mixing your Henrys.

PADDY. No I'm not.

DIGBY. 'My liege I did deny no prisoners' is *Henry IV Part One*. 'But when the blast of war blows in our ears' is *Henry V*.

PADDY. I think I know my –

DIGBY. You see, that's the problem when you get a third at Cambridge, then don't even bother with a training. It's so second rate, Paddy.

   'My liege I did deny no prisoners,
   But I remember when the fight was done,

When I was dry with rage and extreme toil,
Breathless and faint, leaning upon my sword,
Came there a certain lord.'

As opposed to –

'But when the blast of war blows in our ears,
Then imitate the action of the tiger:
Stiffen the sinews, summon up the blood.'

(*To* ROD.) Don't stop, please.

ROD. Wow. I wish I'd seen you.

DIGBY. Bless you. Well, yes, I suppose I'm stuck now in the audio wilderness. Have been for years. I'm a tart, you see. We all are really. Aren't we, gang? We've sold our souls to the proverbial. All in the cause of that filthy 'lucca' we never knew we needed. And now, of course, we're stuck. We're fatally flawed. Mel's being bled dry by the English legal system. Gregory's saving up to get a life, and Paddy – ah, Paddy,'the Pad' –

MEL. Digby –

DIGBY. Well, the Pad's on his third wife so he has to shovel everything into the furnaces of suburbia. He does a very good impression of a banker, don't you think? Why are you so embarrassed by your profession, 'Pad'?

PADDY. Strictly speaking it's not a profession, it's a trade.

DIGBY. I rest my case. Yes. We're all terribly successful.

ROD. I brought this, by the way.

He gives DIGBY *the package.*

DIGBY. Did you? You remembered. That's so kind. (*Opening it.*) Ah yes. Thank you.

ROD. That's cool. It'll be a buzz for me knowing they're playing it on the show.

MEL*'s mobile gives a text alert.*

DIGBY. Yes, it's terribly exciting, isn't it? Daunting and exciting at the same time. How are you set for a voice-over agent, Rod?

ROD. I haven't got one –

DIGBY. Well, why don't I have a word with my girl Sharon at Hudson's? She's very . . . solid.

ROD. Really? Could you?

DIGBY. Yes, of course.

ROD. That would be awesome, thank you –

DIGBY. My pleasure, Rod. Anything to help a struggling young talent. And now's a good time. Because it's quiet, she'll be able to meet you properly.

MEL. How long do you think the strike's going to go on for?

GREG. I give it a week.

DIGBY. It's going to be for as long as it takes.

PADDY. Do you honestly think it'll drag on more than a week?

DIGBY.
'So long as men can breathe or eyes to see,
So long lives this, and this gives life to thee.'

Do you know, they wanted to use that on a cigarette job? In the seventies. They were looking for something upmarket. 'This – (*Puffs.*) gives life to me.' They wanted to put in a 'puff' and take out the 'thee'.

The phone rings and goes straight to answerphone.

Fucking cheek. 'Not with me you're not,' I said.

LILY (MEL*'s daughter, on answerphone*). Mummy, it's me. I'm not feeling very well again, so Daddy said I better stay at home today. And if I'm not feeling any better tomorrow –

MEL (*picking up the receiver*). Hello, darling. What's the matter? Excuse me. Oh dear. Have you? A hundred and one!

MEL goes into the bathroom.

DIGBY. Do you know, I've spent thousands on that foot. They were worried I might lose it altogether.

GREG. Right. Anyone for toast – ?

DIGBY. But I fought like a tiger –

PADDY. Yes please –

DIGBY. Oh, how do you encapsulate your life in eight records? Eight measly slivers of sound.

GREG. Well, I don't think you have to look at it quite like that.

ROD. Why not?

GREG. I'm sorry?

ROD. Why shouldn't you look at it like that?

GREG. Because it's impossible. That's not what the show's about.

ROD. Yes it is. It's about your memories.

DIGBY. Quite.

ROD. The music that reminds you of certain times.

GREG. Well, I don't think the music should have to be that specific.

PADDY. Oh look, Digby, I think it's about time I –

ROD. It's like when you smell a particular smell, it triggers a response, a memory. Why shouldn't that be specific?

GREG. Why should it be? What if it was a crap piece of music? Why shouldn't you just choose music you love? Life's not a science.

MEL *comes out of the bathroom and puts the phone back.*

ROD. Yes it is.

PADDY. Digby? Everyone?

PADDY*'s mobile goes off. He switches it off.*

GREG. No, it's not –

ROD. It's finite. It's a social science.

GREG. Oh, really?

ROD. Why don't you want to pin it down?

GREG. What are you talking about?

ROD. I think that's sitting on the fence.

GREG. It's what?

ROD. It's sitting on the fence.

GREG. Sorry, how old are you?

ROD. This isn't an age thing. This is a life thing.

GREG. Gosh! Is it?

MEL. Greg.

PADDY. Can I just say something – ?

DIGBY. Shut up, Paddy!

PADDY. Fine –

ROD. Can't you define yourself, then?

GREG. It's not about defining yourself.

ROD. Well, I think that's a cop-out.

The phone rings and goes straight to answerphone.

GREG. And I think that the show is about choosing the eight
   pieces of music that would sustain you on a desert island,
   not the musical equivalent of a scratch-and-sniff card –

PADDY. You've burnt the toast.

GREG. Fuck!

BELINDA (*on answerphone*). Paddy, darling, you're switched
   off again and the gardener needs to know where you want
   the new peony trees. Can you just give me a quick tinkle to
   let me know? Bye.

MEL. What about the book, Digby? Is it still the Dickens?

DIGBY. Christ! Don't start me on books. It's completely
impossible. How do you – Oh, I don't want to talk about
books. What would you take, Rod?

ROD. Photos.

DIGBY. Photos?

ROD. Yeah. A photo album, I think.

MEL. Shouldn't that be your luxury?

ROD. It's a book, isn't it?

MEL. Well, strictly speaking –

DIGBY. It's about words, Rod. The importance of . . . You
can't go without words.

ROD. I need pictures.

GREG. You've got it all worked out, then?

ROD. And these are your luxuries?

DIGBY. Oh, it's a mile long.

ROD. Too much choice, you see. It's just baggage.

DIGBY. I know, I know.

ROD. And too much choice is no choice.

PADDY. What a wise head.

GREG. And on such young shoulders.

DIGBY. I was one of the pioneers, you know –

GREG. In the Wild West of Soho.

DIGBY. Bringing artistic credibility to all of this.

PADDY. And the extraordinary thing is, he really believes
that –

DIGBY. At least I believe in something. The only thing that
you believe in is the 18.58 to Guildford.

*ROD's walkie-talkie makes a noise and a scratchy, barely
intelligible voice calls for him.*

ROD. Right, well, I'd better get going.

DIGBY. But you've only just arrived.

ROD. I've got to pay the rent. Thanks for the coffee.

MEL. Pleasure.

DIGBY. Couldn't I pay you to do my foot? You must leave
your number so I can let you know about Fräulein Brauloff.
Why don't you pop round tomorrow? I could take you to
meet her myself.

ROD. I've got an interview for a telly.

DIGBY. Really? Have you? Perfect. You can come on after.
Quick drink with Sharon and then dinner at The Ivy, on me.
If you'd like?

ROD. Awesome. I'll text you.

DIGBY. No you won't. I haven't got a mobile. Can't stand
them.

ROD. Oh, I'm sorry.

DIGBY. You can't e-mail me either because I haven't got a
computer, and I don't want one.

ROD. Here's my card.

DIGBY. Lovely. (*To* GREG.) Put that on for me, would you?
(*To* ROD.) Good luck for the telly. If you need any help . . .

GREG *puts the CD on the hi-fi.* DIGBY *puts the headphones
on.* PADDY *stops* ROD *on the landing, which is out of view
from the flat.*

PADDY. I think I might be able to help you out, vis-à-vis your
rent, if you're interested. It's a bit of voice-over work. Not
affected by the strike. Could be a decent little earner for
you, though.

ROD. Really?

PADDY. Just . . . keep it a bit hush-hush, that's all.

ROD. I have to tell you, I really thought you were awesome as
Hotspur.

PADDY. Oh. Was I?

ROD. You were so . . . You made it all make sense.

PADDY. That's marvellous. Anyway –

ROD. In fact, I wrote to you. I had a massive crush.

PADDY. Did you?

ROD. Yeah.

PADDY. Why don't I walk down with you?

ROD *leaves with* PADDY.

DIGBY. What do you think?

MEL. Very nice.

DIGBY. Really?

MEL. Yes. Very good looking.

DIGBY. Yes, very. Kind of him to bring the recording, wasn't it?

MEL. Very.

DIGBY. He's very like that. Very useful him being a masseur, isn't it?

GREG. So, Digby, were me and Paddy as insufferable as that?

DIGBY. What are you talking about?

GREG. You took me to The Ivy.

DIGBY. Did I?

GREG. Oh, come on –

DIGBY. I can't think why.

GREG. It's the voice tips next, isn't it?

DIGBY. 'Be wise as thou art cruel.'

GREG. When you've got him and his diaphragm right where you want him.

DIGBY *goes to the bathroom.*

What?

MEL. What did you have to do that for?

GREG. It's embarrassing watching him make a fool of himself.

MEL. Oh, go and learn your lines.

GREG *leaves.*

Digby, are you all right?

DIGBY (*off*). Fine. I'm fine.

MEL. I've got some arnica gel. I could put some on if you'd like. To bring down the bruising.

DIGBY *comes out of the bathroom.*

DIGBY. Thank you.

MEL *dabs arnica gel around* DIGBY*'s eye.*

MEL. I use it on the kids.

DIGBY. I picked someone up. On Friday night. First time in years. He was a builder. A big chap. He suddenly turned. Went berserk, actually. For no reason. It was very frightening.

MEL. Oh God.

DIGBY. I couldn't go out. I thought he might be waiting for me. That's why I had to stay here. And now I can't find my keys.

MEL. Oh, Digby. Do you think we should go to the police?

DIGBY. Absolutely not. That's the last thing we need.

MEL. But don't you think –

DIGBY. No. Case closed.

MEL. Do you want to change the locks?

DIGBY. I really don't want the others to know.

MEL. They don't have to.

DIGBY. Do you think we should change the locks?

MEL. If you're worried.

DIGBY. Oh, no. I'll think about it.

MEL. I can tell them I lost my keys. Have you seen a doctor?

DIGBY. No. It's fine. I'm sure it looks much worse than it feels. What am I going to do if Kirsty Young says something on the programme? I'll be so embarrassed.

MEL. She wouldn't. Anyway, we can put some make-up on it.

DIGBY. I suppose so.

MEL. It's not telly. No one's going to see you.

DIGBY. No. God forbid I should ever do any telly, ever again.

MEL. Why didn't you phone me?

DIGBY. I didn't want to bother you.

MEL. You should have.

DIGBY. Not on your weekend with the children. Oh, Mel. Not again?

MEL. She'd booked Center Parcs for the weekend. And he'd forgotten.

DIGBY. Oh no.

MEL. What was I supposed to do? I couldn't be Cruella de Vil and stop them going.

DIGBY. I would have.

MEL. I couldn't.

DIGBY. You bloody should have. Have you ever been to one of those places? I did their TV guff. Unbelievably depressing.

MEL. Not if you're seven and four.

DIGBY. I'm sorry.

MEL. Look, I better go, I've got a session.

DIGBY. Right.

MEL. I'll get you some keys cut.

DIGBY. Thanks.

MEL. Will you be OK?

DIGBY *nods.* MEL *goes.* DIGBY *lifts up his shirt to reveal badly bruised ribs. He takes the arnica gel and starts dabbing it on his body.*

Five

Next day. The flat. The phone rings and goes straight to answerphone.

SHARON (*on answerphone*). Digby? Digby? You have to call me. Gonnadoo? You did a test yesterday. They want to see you again tomorrow. Talking about a six-figure buy-out.

Lights up on the flat. DIGBY *and* PADDY *are putting together the placards and banners.* GREG *is looking at his lines.*

GREG. Six figures –

PADDY. Fuck me sideways.

SHARON (*on answerphone*). They've got to ISDN you to their creatives in Frankfurt, Dallas, Barcelona and –

DIGBY. – Saturn –

SHARON (*on answerphone*). Sydney.

DIGBY. Not far off.

PADDY. That's a lot of creatives.

DIGBY. She uses the term loosely. (*He puts the call on speakerphone.*) I'm not going to do it any differently. Why can't they just play back the bloody tape?

SHARON (*on speakerphone*). Hello, darling. It's the ISDN factor. And, of course, I did remind them about this fucking strike next week. So there is some urgency to wrap this up before then.

DIGBY. Too bloody right there is.

SHARON (*on speakerphone*). Anyway, we'll talk about it later. Is Greg still there?

DIGBY. Yes.

SHARON (*on speakerphone*). I'll see you in the pub, darling. About half an hour.

PADDY *accidentally hits his finger with a hammer.*

DIGBY. Righto.

SHARON (*on speakerphone*). Greg! I've had some comeback from the gel people session that you did last week.

GREG. What?

SHARON (*on speakerphone*). They're not happy, Greg. They're complaining you walked out before they were satisfied.

GREG. What?

SHARON (*on speakerphone*). They're not satisfied.

GREG. I didn't walk out!

He picks up the handset, taking it off speakerphone, and goes to the bathroom.

Sharon, I didn't walk out. That's complete bullshit.

GREG *closes the bathroom door.* PADDY *presses the speakerphone button again.*

SHARON (*on speakerphone*). You kept ignoring their direction, love, so they're not going to pay unless you go back.

GREG (*on speakerphone*). Fuck them, then. They didn't know what they were doing.

SHARON (*on speakerphone*). Please don't do this, Greg. They want you to do the session again. This afternoon at five.

GREG (*on speakerphone*). I can't. Not this afternoon.

SHARON (*on speakerphone*). This is getting really boring, Greg. I'll have to get back to you.

GREG (*on speakerphone*). What?

SHARON (*on speakerphone*). I'll have to get back to you.
(*She hangs up.*)

GREG (*on speakerphone*). Sharon? Sharon?

*PADDY turns the speakerphone off. GREG comes out of
the bathroom and puts the phone back. PADDY holds up
one of the banners. It reads: 'No to Dolly! No to the Dolly
voice!'*

PADDY. What do we think?

DIGBY. 'No to Dolly! No to the Dolly voice!'

PADDY. Exactly.

DIGBY. 'No to Dolly! No to the Dolly voice'? Paddy, am
I missing something profound and interesting?

PADDY. You remember Dolly?

DIGBY. Dolly?

PADDY. Dolly the sheep. 'No to a cloned sheep. No to a
cloned voice.'

The placard falls off its battening.

Bugger!

DIGBY. So that's what you're going to be chanting, is it?
Could get a bit lost on the barricades, Pad. (*To* GREG.)
Where's yours?

*GREG holds up his banner which reads 'We're fucked.
We're all fucked. Because of you!'*

GREG. What? Does exactly what it says on the tin. Can we
just . . . you know? One last time. Just to . . . you know –

DIGBY. Come on then. With feeling.

DIGBY and PADDY each pick up a piece of paper.

'You gotta let him in, Pat,'

GREG. 'Please. Let me speak to her. Pat, it's Michael. Michael
Brennan from the church.'

PADDY. 'I can't. What's the point? I'm not coming out.'

GREG. 'Pat. I'm not going to try and stop you. I just want to talk to you.'

DIGBY. 'You've gotta give it up, Pat. It ain't worth it. Come on, let's talk about it. Just put the gun down.'

GREG. 'Let me talk to her on my own for a minute. Please.'

DIGBY (*prompting*). '. . . I just want to talk to you, Pat – '

GREG. Fuck! 'Let me talk to her on my own for a minute. Please. I just want to talk to you, Pat.'

PADDY. 'Go away. There's nothing you can do that's going to stop me.'

DIGBY (*prompting*). ' . . . I know how you feel – '

GREG. Yes, I know. I'm just pausing. I'm finding the thought. OK?

DIGBY. Right –

GREG. Can we just . . . ? I've completely lost my thread now.

DIGBY. Sorry.

PADDY (*prompting*). ' . . . I know how you feel – '

GREG. 'I know how you feel. I've been desperate in my life, too, and in that desperation I found God's love. Just let me come in, Pat. Please.'

PADDY. 'You promise you won't try anything.'

GREG. What?

PADDY. 'You promise you won't try anything?'

GREG. Paddy, you're mumbling.

PADDY. No I'm not.

GREG. Can you just speak up a bit, please?

PADDY. 'You promise you won't try anything!'

GREG. 'I promise. You can trust me. God won't let you down.'

The phone rings.

'He won't turn his back on you, Pat. I've been there. Where you are now. Rock bottom. And I've come out the other – '

TOM (*on answerphone*). Mel. Do you ever switch your phone on? I've seen the solicitor and he says I'm the main carer, so the court won't want to disrupt the kids' stability, all right? There's absolutely no point in you –

During this we hear MEL *coming up the stairs. She enters and picks up the phone.*

MEL. I've been working, Tom. I said, I've been working. The strike hasn't . . . Yeah, that is the point, and I'm prepared to stop working like this so I can be with them. Yes! Altogether if I have to. Because I'd like to be the main carer! You'll have to sell a few paintings, then. Well, get a fucking job. (*Puts phone down.*) Sorry about that.

She goes into the kitchen and pours a glass of wine.

GREG. 'I've come out the other side.'

PADDY. 'Stay away from me or I'll shoot.'

GREG. 'You won't shoot me, Pat. Now, give me the gun.' (*Beat.*) How was that?

DIGBY. Well, with a bit of polishing on the way over.

PADDY. Yes, tighten it up. Give it a good polish on the way over.

GREG. I thought I'd wear this.

PADDY. Yes, very good.

GREG. What?

PADDY. Very pastoral.

GREG. Right. (*Beat.*) Is it?

MEL. You look great. Good luck!

GREG. Thank you.

DIGBY. Yes, knock 'em dead.

PADDY. We'll be doing some serious praying for you.

DIGBY. 'Once more unto the breach . . . '

    GREG *nods and goes.*

    Is he all right?

PADDY. Deaf as a post. Doesn't stand a chance.

DIGBY. Yes, what is wrong with him? Mel, do you know
    what's wrong with Greg?

PADDY. Nerves.

MEL. I think he just needs to get his ears syringed.

DIGBY. And what on earth was that accent?

PADDY. Well, I had an interesting chat with Memphis this
    morning. Stratford have offered me a very nice line of parts
    in the next season.

    MEL *comes out of the kitchen with a bottle of wine and*
    some glasses.

DIGBY. You're joking. Which parts?

PADDY. Caesar in *Antony and Cleopatra*, Polixenes in *The*
    Winter's Tale, and there's a new play as well.

DIGBY. Really?

MEL. A new play as well.

PADDY. That's where we met. *Winter's Tale*. Do you remember?

DIGBY. Course I remember.

PADDY. My first job.

DIGBY. 'We are but plain fellows, sir.'

PADDY. 'A lie; you are rough and hairy.'

DIGBY. So are you going to do it, then?

PADDY. Well . . .

    The phone rings.

MEL. You could get very poncy and tell Sharon it's a sabbatical.

BELINDA (*on answerphone*). Hello, darling, you're switched off. Will you be on the 18.58? It would be lovely because we've got Kiki and Paul coming –

PADDY (*picks up the phone, then pours himself a glass of wine*). Hello, darling. I'm afraid they're running awfully late my end. I know. Just ISDN-ing now. (*Takes a sip.*) Yup. Soon as. (*Puts the phone back.*) Of course I'd love to go back to Stratford.

DIGBY. Would you?

PADDY. Yes. But . . . I've got to be realistic.

DIGBY. Really? Why start now?

PADDY. It just doesn't pay the school fees.

DIGBY. Are you paying for the whole fucking school now?

PADDY. You'd be surprised what a dent three sets of school fees makes.

DIGBY. When was the last time you went on stage?

PADDY. Here we go.

DIGBY. It's not difficult, Paddy, when was it? And I'm not including that *Whoops No Mrs* rubbish you did on tour –

PADDY. Why not? It wasn't rubbish –

MEL / DIGBY. It was rubbish –

PADDY. A lot of people really enjoyed that –

DIGBY. A lot of people really enjoy slot machines.

PADDY. Did you see the reviews?

DIGBY. Not the *Preston Echo*, no. Just admit it, you're scared. You're losing your hair, the body's . . . Well, you're not the beautiful boy any more, are you – ?

PADDY. So you keep telling me!

DIGBY. And the bottle's gone. Hasn't it? Dried up.

MEL. Digby, I don't think that's really –

PADDY. You're jealous.

DIGBY. Course I'm jealous. No one's offering me Caesar and Polixenes. I get offered MFI and Mr fucking Sheen! What the hell happened to you, Paddy? You had all the big guns. What is it? Is it the lines? The memory? It's not just about the money, is it? Not any more. Say something! Tell me it's not the money. Tell me I'm wrong. Please tell me I'm wrong!

PADDY *leaves*.

I wake up each morning thinking, is this it? Is this the extent of it? I haven't done anything worth talking about.

MEL. We're all going to be forgotten, Digby.

DIGBY. You have children, Mel.

There is a knock at the door. DIGBY *opens it.*

Wow! You look a million dollars.

ROD. Thanks.

DIGBY. Come in. I've booked us a table at The Ivy.

ROD. Awesome. Thanks.

DIGBY. My treat. Wow. He looks like a movie star. Doesn't he, Mel?

MEL. Yes. He does.

ROD. Thank you. So do you. (*Referring to the banners.*) Looking good.

DIGBY. Isn't it?

He picks up a banner and gives it to ROD.

I've earmarked this one for you.

ROD. Excellent.

DIGBY. The Dean Street cell. Shoulder to shoulder.

ROD. Awesome.

DIGBY. Yes. Well, we better be off.

DIGBY *goes into the bathroom.*

ROD. OK.

DIGBY (*off*). We're meeting Sharon first. Get the business end out of the way.

ROD. Right. (*Beat, then in an American accent.*) Take your glasses off, Miss Jones, you're beautiful.

DIGBY *comes out of the bathroom.*

DIGBY. Night-night, then.

MEL. Yup.

ROD. Goodnight.

MEL. Have a nice time.

ROD *and* DIGBY *leave.* MEL *pours another drink. Lights fade.*

Six

DIGBY *bursts through the door with* ROD. *They are dancing together.* ROD *leads* DIGBY *around with spins and turns.*

ROD. Wait, wait, wait.

ROD *goes to the piles of music, chooses a CD and puts it on.*

DIGBY. Christ, I'm still spinning.

ROD. That's the idea. It's not difficult, right?

DIGBY. What is it again?

A jive track begins, and they start to dance again. ROD *leads* DIGBY.

ROD. It's a mixture of jive and salsa. It's fun, isn't it?

DIGBY. It's wonderful.

ROD. It's ceroc.

DIGBY. Se-what?

ROD. Ceroc. From the French.

DIGBY. Why have I never done this before?

ROD. You're a natural.

DIGBY. Rubbish. I'm awful. But I don't give a toss. I love it.

DIGBY *loses his balance and falls on the sofa.* ROD *flings himself down next to him.*

That was wonderful.

ROD. Are you OK?

DIGBY. What?

ROD. Are you . . . ?

ROD *uses the remote control to fade the music to a lower level.* DIGBY *finds his keys down the side of the sofa.* ROD *hooks up his iPod to the hi-fi speakers, and puts on a piece of electronic music.*

DIGBY. I thought I'd lost these.

ROD. I'll take you. Next time I go. Ceroc night.

ROD *gets down on the floor and takes* DIGBY's *shoes and socks off.*

DIGBY. You'd take me? Would you?

ROD. Yeah.

ROD *massages* DIGBY's *feet.*

DIGBY. Oh, that's wonderful.

ROD. What do you think of this music?

DIGBY. Um, well . . . It's, er . . .

ROD. It's one of mine.

DIGBY. Is it? Gosh.

ROD. I compose a bit. iGarage.

DIGBY. Quite. Lovely.

ROD. So we got to record number four.

DIGBY. Yes. Where was I?

ROD. Under the spell of Richard Burton.

DIGBY. Ah yes. Trying to get a voice like Burton's. Standing on the side of a windy mountain and screaming blue murder to rip away at the larynx.

ROD. You have very interesting feet, do you know that?

DIGBY. They're plates of meat. Ugly things.

ROD. No. That's where you're wrong. They're handsome. I read feet.

DIGBY. You read feet?

ROD. As part of the massage thing. I've always had an instinct around feet.

DIGBY. Have you?

ROD. You can tell a lot about someone by the way they've treated their feet. Caring. Respectful. State of the nails. If they smell.

DIGBY. Oh God, they don't smell, do they?

ROD. No, they're lovely feet. Most people just ignore them. See them as . . . 'plates of meat'. Cover them up. I want to celebrate them. After all, they carry us.

DIGBY. Go on, then. What does that foot say about me?

ROD. It says . . . passionate. Sensitive. Interesting.

DIGBY. Oh.

ROD. You'll have to smuggle me onto the island as your Man Friday. (*Beat.*) Do you think . . .

DIGBY. What?

ROD. No. It's all right.

DIGBY. Tell me.

ROD. Do you think I've got a good voice? I mean, should I go and stand on a mountain and do some screaming?

DIGBY. No, no, no, you don't need to do any of that.

ROD. Really?

DIGBY. You've got a lovely voice.

ROD. D'you think so?

DIGBY. Yes. You mustn't do anything to it.

> ROD *puts his head in* DIGBY*'s lap.*

ROD. But has it . . .

DIGBY. What?

ROD. No.

DIGBY. Please.

ROD. Has it . . . Have I got what it takes?

DIGBY. Of course you have.

ROD. I mean, to make it. To really make it.

DIGBY. You have a wonderful quality. Don't think too much about it.

ROD. It's great to talk to you like this. I don't really have anyone else I can share it with.

DIGBY. Sharon loves you, by the way.

ROD. Does she?

DIGBY. You're a hit.

ROD. Am I?

DIGBY. Why don't you take these? They're for here. In case you need a refuge during the day.

> DIGBY *gives* ROD *the keys.*

ROD. I don't know what to say. Are you sure?

DIGBY. Well, it's awfully draining just hanging around otherwise. Between your deliveries. You may as well wait here. And as of next week, we'll all be on the picket line. You'll need a bolt-hole.

ROD. That'd be awesome.

DIGBY. It's what it's for.

ROD. What about the others?

DIGBY. Oh, don't worry about the others. I'll talk to them.
I do worry about you racing around on that thing all day.

ROD. Thank you so much. This is just . . . I don't want to
impose on you, though. Please tell me when you've had
enough. I just love spending time with you.

DIGBY. Not at all.

ROD (*sees* DIGBY*'s watch*). Shit, I've got to go, Digby.

DIGBY. What?

ROD. I'm meeting someone at Groucho's.

DIGBY. Oh. What, now?

ROD. He's proposing me to be a member.

DIGBY. I see. I could propose you to be a member.

ROD. I'd better not be late.

DIGBY. No. Of course not. Shall I hang on for you?

ROD. No, don't worry. It'll probably be a late one.

DIGBY. Oh, right. OK. I've got a big session first thing
anyway. I'll walk over there with you. I can go that way to
the station. Those cats will be wondering where I am.

ROD. Don't worry. I've got to run. Bye.

ROD *leaves.* DIGBY *follows him to the door, grasping his
side.*

DIGBY. Ring me! Let me know how it goes.

Seven

DIGBY *is in a spotlight.*

DIGBY. You're so lucky today. You don't have to remember.
Some machine will do it for you. A vision, a sound, or
memory, captured. I can't remember my father's voice.
There is no voice when I see the pictures in my head.
My father was . . . a difficult person to know, I suppose.
He wasn't able to . . . I don't remember his touch. Except in
anger. He never hit me with his hands. It was always with
his belt. Creases in the leather where he rolled it up and
the tongue curled away from the buckle. I'd look up to it
around his waist. Before he pulled it through the loops. The
belt had been his father's, and he'd taken it off a dead sailor
after a poker fight in Montego Bay. He had a lot of stories
like that. I never quite knew where the truth ran out and
the tales began. I don't think he did either. Well, when I was
ten I was accepted for the grammar. We had no money.
And I rushed home to tell him the news, but he wasn't
there. Mother wasn't there either, of course, she was
working in the shop. I knew where he'd be, though, and
I ran all the way there, all uphill to the allotments. Straight
up to the shed. But as soon as I put my hand on the handle
I knew something was wrong. Did I know that something
was wrong? Did I? I don't know. He'd used the belt, you
see. From the corner joist. I was so breathless from the run
that I . . . stopped breathing. I'd stopped breathing. The
inward breath had stabbed me and it wouldn't come back
out. I couldn't make it come back out and I didn't speak
for nearly a year. After that. You see, Kirsty, for nearly a
year I had no voice at all and this record reminds me of . . .
I can't tell Kirsty Young that.

Eight

ROD *lets himself into the flat, puts on some music, gets a beer from the fridge and lights a spliff. He texts someone. His BlackBerry rings.*

ROD. Yeah, it's groovy. Come on up. 72 Dean Street. It's Scott. Second floor. I'll buzz you up.

Nine

DIGBY *is in a studio. The other people we only hear.*

DIGBY. 'Gonnadoo.'

STEVE (*sound engineer*). Sorry, can I just get a bit for level?

DIGBY. Right. Gonnadoo it here, Gonnadoo it right, Gonnadoo it now –

STEVE. That's great. Thank you.

DIGBY. Gonnadoo's shite. Ready? 'Gonnadoo. For those that are.'

STEVE. Sorry, can we just do an ident first, please?

DIGBY. Why?

STEVE. For the ISDN to the foreign creatives.

DIGBY. Haven't they heard the first one?

STEVE. There's more of them listening this time.

DIGBY. God help us. More 'creatives'? I see. Digby Scott –

STEVE. Hang on. (*Beat.*) When you're ready.

DIGBY. Digby Scott.

STEVE. And agent?

DIGBY. Christ Almighty! Digby Scott with Sharon Brauloff at Hudson's. Forty-four, thirty-six, forty-nine. Star sign Taurus and my hobbies are working with arseholes and masturbation.

STEVE. We're on line now, so do you want to take it from the top?

DIGBY. Yes, lets give it a whirl. 'Gonnadoo. For those that are.' Are what? I think I'm missing a bit.

STEVE. Which bit?

DIGBY. Well, if I knew that then I wouldn't be asking, would I? I would deduce from this that it's the end. 'For those that are.' Are what?

STEVE. No. That's it.

DIGBY. What do you mean, 'That's it'? It doesn't make sense.

STEVE. Hang on a second.

DIGBY. In fact, the whole fucking thing doesn't make sense. 'In Gonnadoo did Kubla Khan a stately pleasure dome decree – '

VOICE 3. Hello, Mr Scote. I am Jose-Luis in Barcelona. I am working on Gonnadoo here for Europe.

DIGBY. Yes.

VOICE 3. Hi. We're listening on the ISDN –

DIGBY. Are you? Good.

VOICE 3. Yes, please, and we're very happy with your voice for this campaign. He is very certain. Completely in his place. We liking if you make him more magical in his colours.

DIGBY. Yes.

VOICE 3. We don't know who he is. He is everyone and nowhere.

DIGBY. Right.

VOICE 3. Under your head. In the floor. He could be the micro . . . micro – *¿Como se dice micro-ondas?* – He is from the microwave . . . maybe. Or not at all.

DIGBY. I see. And you want me to give you that sense of the unknown with this?

VOICE 3. Exacto. That is exactly right. He has the darkness of mystery.

DIGBY. OK. (*To himself.*) It's the blind leading the fucking blind.

VOICE 3. He sees everything. All of everyone –

DIGBY. Righto.

VOICE 3. He is 'Gonnadoo'.

DIGBY. Do what?

VOICE 3. Exactly him.

DIGBY. Of course he is. And are you aware that it doesn't make sense?

VOICE 3. Which?

DIGBY. Grammatically.

VOICE 3. Is which one?

DIGBY. 'For those that are.'

VOICE 3. Yes?

DIGBY. Well, in the English language, my old fruit, we tend to be needing a subject, object and a verb for a sentence to be making sense, otherwise no one will understand.

VOICE 3. If they don't understand he may be a good thing for this enigma.

DIGBY. How can it be, my old china? It has no second half. Do you understand? *Niente secunda.*

VOICE 4. Hello, Mr Scott. This is Ian Campbell in Sydney.

DIGBY. Christ, you're up late.

VOICE 4. 'Fraid so. Big campaign, deadlines, that sort of thing, and it's the voice we're after right now.

DIGBY. Just as a matter of interest, then, so that I can give it what's required, could you enlighten me as to what exactly is meant by 'it'.

VOICE 4. How do you mean?

DIGBY. I do apologise. In plain English, what the fuck does 'Gonnadoo. For those that are' mean?

VOICE 4. Well . . . for those that are 'Gonnadoo it', they can do it . . . If they . . . Sorry, that's not right. If they are 'Gonnadoo it', then they can do it when they 'Gonnadoo it'. No, that's not right either. It's not difficult. If the internet user is using the Gonnadoo search engine, then, er . . . Oh fuck, it's been a long day, mate. Do you reckon you could just give us the line?

DIGBY. 'For those that are.'

VOICE 4. Yeah, I wouldn't worry about the final script, it's going to have massive amounts of global input. They'll dress it up. Give it a bow tie. But if you can just get the voice light and quizzical with plenty of irony that would be perf.

DIGBY. Light and quizzical?

VOICE 4. Yeah. Basically 'gloves off'. That's what the client's after. There'll obviously be the continental specifics. I'm sure the Americans will want it a bit taller.

DIGBY. Oh, I'm sure. With a big fat arse on the end.

VOICE 4. It's the global voice we're after. The 'Oneness of Gonnadoo.' That's the concept. And they know they want an English voice, male, neutral accent, high status and open.

DIGBY. Right, open. Light and quizzical, then, with a bit of high status and dark mystery thrown in.

VOICE 4. If you could. Nothing fancy. And don't go all lovey.

DIGBY. God forbid. (*Beat.*) 'Gonnadoo. For those that are.'

VOICE 4. That's nice.

DIGBY. 'Gonnadoo. For those that are.'

VOICE 3. Hello. Mr Scote. Very nice from Barcelona. Again please, with golden colours from a tunnel.

DIGBY. Right. 'Gonnadoo. For those that are.'

VOICE 3. No, no, no. It was . . .

DIGBY. Too much gold?

VOICE 3. No, not too much, but I want to think of gold over his rainbow.

DIGBY. 'Gonnadoo. For those that are.'

VOICE 3. Yes. Exactly right.

VOICE 4. Yeah, that was nice.

VOICE 3. Completely different. I saw his rainbow. Beautiful.

VOICE 4. Can you wait there for a few moments while we play that back to Tokyo?

DIGBY *makes a paper plane from the script.*

DIGBY. 'To begin at the beginning. It is spring, moonless night in the small town, starless and bible-black, the cobble streets silent and the hunched – '

VOICE 4. Hello, Mr Scott –

DIGBY. Yes.

VOICE 4. Right. We've just been having a brief confab at our end and we've got a few more voices to hear, obviously, but we're very keen as you may be able to tell.

DIGBY. I see. Good.

VOICE 4. There are a few question marks, though.

DIGBY. Oh dear.

VOICE 4. One of which is your union's bloody strike.

DIGBY. Yes.

VOICE 4. And that could potentially really fuck things up for us. So we're wondering what your take is on all that.

DIGBY. My take?

VOICE 4. Yeah. Will you be going on strike next week? 'Cause obviously, if you are, that would affect things.

Silence.

VOICE 3. Mr Scote. Speed is of the moment because of the marketplace, but we will not be conclusive until next week.

VOICE 4. I mean this is too big a deal to get fucked up over a strike. Isn't it? We are talking about a three-year exclusivity deal. It'd probably lead to a visual as well. You would be the main man in every trade paper and glossy from here to Timbuktu. Gonnadoo is offering you global media immortality with this. Fuck it, you'd be able to go and sit on God's right hand by the time the PR queens have finished with you. Well, do we have a deal?

End of Act One.

ACT TWO

One

Blackout.

The following week. First day of the strike.

MEL. I saw you looking at me in the bar.

ROD. I followed you.

MEL. I know.

ROD. The door was open.

MEL. So am I.

ROD. What are you waiting for?

MEL. What was that? I heard a noise.

GREG. What the hell's going on?

MEL. It's my husband.

ROD. Your husband?

> *Lights up on a studio.* MEL, ROD, *and* GREG *are looking at monitors and recording. We don't see* PADDY *to begin with, as he is in the control booth.*

MEL. This is such a nice big one, though. It'd be a shame to see it go to waste.

GREG. OK, baby. But half each, you know the rules.

MEL. D'you like my puppies?

ROD. Yeah, they look like they need a bone to chew on.

MEL. You can stroke them if you want. Ooh yeah. That feels good.

ROD. So does your little pussy.

MEL. I groomed her just this morning. You're so big. Yes. Oh yeah.

GREG. Look at her ring. Isn't it cute?

ROD. It's a beauty.

GREG. I've got just the thing for that. Make some room, baby. I want to make a sandwich.

MEL. One for my pussy and one for my little ring. Ding-a-ling. Just the way I like it.

GREG. A double-decker. Nice.

GREG*'s mobile gets a text alert. He gets it out and looks at the message.*

PADDY (*off*). For Christ's sake!

GREG. Sorry. Sorry, everyone. Sorry, Pad.

PADDY (*off*). Mobiles off. Please. And you've got to stay consistent with a level.

GREG. I am.

PADDY *comes in and fiddles with* GREG*'s mic.*

PADDY. You're too bloody loud.

GREG. No I'm not.

PADDY. I set a level, then you go off mic. Then you're popping to buggery.

GREG. I've got a cold. I'm bunged up.

PADDY. You don't sound bunged up.

GREG. Well, I am.

PADDY *leaves the booth.*

MEL. Are you OK?

GREG. I'm fine.

MEL. Who was that?

GREG. Sorry. I thought it was going to be . . . them.

PADDY (*off*). Melanie?

MEL. Paddy?

PADDY (*off*). Can you give it another come there?

MEL. Where?

PADDY (*off*). There. Just give it another come.

MEL. What? For the double penetration?

PADDY (*off*). Yup.

MEL. You want her coming during that?

PADDY (*off*). Yes, please.

MEL. Paddy, have you ever come during a double penetration?

PADDY (*off*). Oh, don't start on that again. Just do it, will you? Pretend she's S and M. Right. Now pick it up from the first cock going in. And Greg, please try and sound more interested. Remember, this comes straight after all the goldicocks stuff. I'll drop you in.

The tape plays again.

GREG (*recorded*). Make some room, baby. I want to make a sandwich.

MEL. One for my pussy and one for my little ring. Ding-a-ling. Just the way I like it. (*She comes.*)

GREG. A double-decker. Nice.

PADDY (*off*). Hold it. Sorry. I've got a problem this end.

GREG. Come on.

ROD. Do you do many of these, then?

MEL. Yes, but don't say anything to Digby. He'd be horrified.

GREG *texts a message and puts the mobile on silent.*

PADDY (*voice-over*). 'On or off road, you'll never drive anything smoother. This is the ride of your – '

(*Off.*) Oh, Rod.

ROD. Yeah?

PADDY (*off*). Careful with the popping.

MEL. Don't get too close to the mic.

ROD. Oh right.

PADDY (*off*). Nice and amateur, though.

ROD. Oh yeah, sure. (*To* MEL.) What?

MEL. The punters like it apparently. Sounds more authentic.

GREG. Less dubbed.

ROD. But it is dubbed.

MEL. You'll get used to it. Just think of the money.

PADDY (*voice-over*). 'On or off road, you'll never drive anything smoother – '

(*Off.*) No, no, no. Sorry. Got a glitch. What the hell have I done?

ROD (*voice-over*). 'Ooh yeah, baby, I'm going to huff and I'm going to puff and I'm going to blow you right off.'

MEL (*voice-over*). 'Not by the hairs on my quimmy-quim-quim.'

PADDY (*off*). Sorry about this.

MEL. He likes to do it all. Mixing. Effects. It's a bit of a hobby, isn't it?

GREG. What?

MEL. I said it's Paddy's thing.

GREG. Is it fuck! He's just too tight to pay an engineer.

PADDY (*off*). OK, problem solved. Now pick it up from 'a double-decker, nice'. Bit of improvisation before the cue line, please. I'll drop it in. Thank you.

GREG. 'A double-decker. Nice.'

They improvise, waiting for GREG, *who is checking his messages again. The tape stops again.*

PADDY (*off*). For Christ's sake, Greg! You've got another line there.

GREG. Where?

PADDY (*off*). There.

GREG. Does it really matter?

PADDY (*off*). Yes it does. That's how they get the dog on.

GREG. The dog?

MEL. What dog – ?

PADDY (*off*). Come on, guys, we haven't got time. Just do it –

MEL. Paddy, we've talked about this before.

PADDY (*off*). It's not a big dog.

GREG. Oh, for fuck's sake.

PADDY (*off*). Look, I haven't got time for this.

GREG. Neither have I, I've got to go.

MEL. What do you mean, you've 'got to go'?

GREG *gets up and collects his stuff.* PADDY *comes into the studio.*

GREG. He's overrun. You booked me for an hour and now I've got to go.

PADDY. You can't go.

GREG. I'm going.

PADDY. I booked you. You're booked.

GREG. Is there overtime?

PADDY. I promised Gunter we'd –

GREG. You've had your hour, Paddy –

PADDY. You're the reason we've been overrunning.

GREG. Rubbish.

PADDY. That bloody mobile –

GREG. Well, I am waiting for a rather life-changing piece of news –

PADDY. You've been on and off the mic like a sodding yo-yo. / Where are you going?

GREG. I don't have to tell you where I'm going.

PADDY. Well, I want to know.

GREG. I'm not telling you.

PADDY. Are you doing another job?

This stops GREG *in his tracks.*

MEL. Christ Almighty, Greg! You're not, are you?

GREG. I've got to. It's Gillette.

PADDY. You're breaking the strike?

MEL. It's the first day, Greg!

GREG. It's my Gillette!

MEL. You can't.

GREG. It's their fault. It was meant to be last week.

PADDY (*to* ROD). You're not hearing this.

MEL. Does Sharon know?

GREG. Of course she knows. Technically, she's putting it through as last week.

PADDY. Oh, right. I see.

MEL. Jesus.

GREG. I'm not the only one.

MEL. What if Pig finds out? They'll make your name stink. No one'll touch you.

GREG. Don't you understand? This isn't a game. If I don't do it, I'll lose the gig altogether and I can't afford to do that. I've got to pay the rent!

MEL (*to herself*). We've all got to do that.

GREG *leaves.*

Well this is all very exciting. On your first session.

PADDY. Marvellous! Fan-fucking-tastic! Your commitment very much appreciated. Well, we can't do any more now. Can you do tomorrow?

ROD. Awesome gig, yeah.

MEL. OK. Text me a time. I better get back to the picket line.

PADDY. Thanks, darling.

He hands MEL *some cash as she leaves.*

See you there. That was good, Rod. Very amateur. Just right.

ROD. Oh.

PADDY. House style. 'Buttman, Screw Your Neighbour.' Everyone wants it next-door-ish. Wobbly camera, wobbly bits.

ROD. By the way, did you manage to have that word with your agent?

PADDY. Sorry? Oh yes. Of course. Memphis. I meant to ring him.

ROD. I don't want to pester you.

PADDY. Not at all. I'll do it today.

ROD. Awesome.

PADDY. It was a ton, wasn't it?

As they leave.

ROD. Do you fancy a drink?

PADDY. Why not?

ROD. And maybe a sandwich?

PADDY. I beg your pardon?

ROD. A double-decker.

PADDY. Oh yes! Course.

Blackout.

Two

Early evening. ROD *is about to enter the flat when he hears* SHARON *on the answerphone and listens outside the open door.* DIGBY *has his donkey jacket on and is a bit feverish.*

SHARON (*on answerphone*). Digby? Please can you call me back? I'm at home. I've got to talk to you. I just don't know what to do. Gonnadoo have been on the phone again. They've heard everyone. How can you turn this down? I think you're making a huge mistake. Deals like this don't just come and go. And you're not going to win this strike.

DIGBY (*to himself*). Yes we bloody are.

SHARON (*on answerphone*). I know you've been on the picket line, but it's ridiculous I can't get hold of you. Please let me give you a mobile phone, Digby! I'm leaving another message on the home number. If you call me when you get this there could still be time. I don't think they know what they want now. Call me, Digby, please. I'm worried about you.

ROD *enters with a carrier bag. In it are scented candles, champagne and Nurofen Plus.*

ROD. Digby? I'm really, really, sorry. It was . . . it was amazing today, wasn't it? A real picket line! In the square!

DIGBY. Where were you?

ROD. I know. I got completely . . .

DIGBY. . . . what?

ROD. If only you had a mobile I could have texted you. Mel told me you weren't feeling too good.

DIGBY. It's just a bit of a chill. Standing around.

ROD (*getting out the painkillers*). Do you want these with water? (*Gets out the bottle.*) Or champagne?

DIGBY. I've had some.

ROD. Please stay. A few minutes.

DIGBY. No. I've got to go home, Rod, I'm not –

ROD *takes* DIGBY *by the hands and leads him to the sofa.*

ROD. Oh, Digby! Please. Five minutes. Don't go. I've got a surprise. National television news, Digby. We made the news.

DIGBY. Did we?

ROD. We were so gutted you weren't there. It was just after you'd left. I must have just missed you. Literally. It was a sound bite, OK, but we've got to see the news. The camera came in really close. And the reporter was – You'd know him, he was so intense. His eyebrows were amazingly supportive. And we played this new anthem I've written. And he said, 'What is it?' And I said I composed it for the strike.

ROD *puts his composed piece on the hi-fi, and gets out some scented candles from his carrier bag.*

On my iPod and Pig's car speakers, which are amazing, in the square. Can you imagine it? The sound bouncing off the walls of the square and there's hundreds of people now. There's us. And the camera crew and . . . He's so cool, Pig, isn't he? And the reporter wants a copy of the piece, isn't that awesome? So does Pig. I said I'd burn it for them. And now he's talking about – wait for this – doing a news feature on us.

DIGBY. What?

ROD. Well, on you mostly. Because I said that . . . Well, I said that the anthem was inspired . . . by you.

DIGBY. Really? Was it?

ROD. Yeah. Ah. It's just so amazing, this strike. So I bought this to celebrate. And I'd like to dedicate it to you.

ROD *kisses* DIGBY *on the lips.*

Thank you, Digby. I just want to say . . . I think you're awesome.

Three

DIGBY *is in a spotlight.* ROD*'s anthem underscores.*

DIGBY. Well, Kirsty . . . I never dreamed that this would
    happen so late in my life. But yes, it has, unbelievably. Of
    course, my partner's very much younger than me, and people
    sometimes take him for my son. Which is embarrassing . . .
    more for me than him. Oh, he's remarkably comfortable
    with it. So tell me about your next piece of music? Well,
    Kirsty, this is a piece of music he wrote and I'd like very
    much to have it on the island with me.

Four

A week later. The flat. Early evening. MEL *has her mobile on
loudspeaker on the coffee table as she opens a bottle of wine
and pours a glass. She has piles of legal papers and documents
spread out. She talks to her daughter, Lily.*

LILY (*on speakerphone*). And we did three laps all the way
    round the edge of the common.

MEL. Three laps!

LILY (*on speakerphone*). All the way round three times, which
    is six miles.

MEL. Lily, you did six miles?

LILY (*on speakerphone*). Yes.

MEL. Are you sure it was six miles?

LILY (*on speakerphone*). Yes!

MEL. You must be exhausted.

LILY (*on speakerphone*). I was quite tired at the end. Maeve
    and Harry were tireder.

MEL. I should think you were. I didn't realise you were doing
    six miles.

LILY (*on speakerphone*). I was only going to go round once, but Stacy said I could carry on with her and do the whole thing if I wasn't tired.

MEL. Where was Daddy?

LILY (*on speakerphone*). He only did three miles. He joined it half way. Stacy thinks he's lazy.

MEL. I think that was far too much for you, darling.

LILY (*on speakerphone*). So that's six pounds you owe me for the cancer charity. Will you bring it on Friday?

MEL. Of course I will.

LILY (*on speakerphone*). And I'll show you my room before we go, OK? It's two different purples now. A lighter one and a darker one, but not too dark. And Dad's going to make a frame for my certificate from the walk to say I did it.

MEL. Is he? That's great.

LILY (*on speakerphone*). I've got to go now, Mum, we're having supper.

MEL. OK. Can I have a quick word with Daddy?

LILY (*on speakerphone*). He's not here.

MEL. Where is he?

LILY (*on speakerphone*). I don't know. Do you want to speak to Stacy?

MEL. That's all right. I'll talk to him later.

LILY (*on speakerphone*). OK. Stacy wants to know how the strike's going.

MEL. Well . . . er, yes, it's still going.

LILY (*on speakerphone*). Coming! Bye, Mummy.

MEL. I'll ring you tomorrow –

LILY (*on speakerphone*). Bye.

MEL. Bye-bye, darling.

Silence. MEL *goes into the bathroom*. ROD *lets himself in. He is in a donkey jacket and carries a rucksack. He puts some music on the hi-fi and starts to undress. He gets his shirt and jeans out of the rucksack.*

MEL *comes out of the bathroom.*

ROD. Oh. Hi.

MEL. Hello.

ROD. Sorry, I didn't realise you were here. Hope you don't mind. Digby lent me a key.

MEL. Did he?

ROD. I've got an audition. He said I could use the flat, if that's OK. I wanted to get changed.

MEL. Oh, right.

ROD. There is an iron, isn't there?

MEL. It's, er . . . under the sink.

ROD. It's for a movie.

MEL. Really?

ROD. Yeah. I want to make an impression. You know.

MEL. It's a bit late for an audition, isn't it?

ROD. I know. The director's flying back to LA in the morning. They're seeing me specially this evening.

ROD *sets up the ironing board, etc.*

Do you mind if I take a shower?

MEL. No. Go ahead. Towels on the side.

ROD. I've just been on the picket line.

MEL. Whitfield Street?

ROD. Yeah. Where were you?

MEL. In the square, then I had to see my lawyer, you know.

ROD. Woah, that looks like some pretty heavy shit.

MEL. Yeah, very heavy.

ROD. You really miss your kids, don't you? (*Beat.*) I bet you're a lovely mum.

MEL. Anyway . . .

ROD *goes to the bathroom, leaving the door open.*

ROD. When I left, Pig and Digby were filling this huge metal bin with bits of wood. I think they were going to set fire to it.

The shower goes on.

MEL. Really?

ROD. Like the firemen.

MEL. Are people heckling them?

ROD. Not any more. They're having a whale of a time. T h e r e 's a whole crowd now, watching them. Star-spotting. The performing picket line. (*Imitating* DIGBY.) 'No to Dolly! No to the Dolly voice!' Here's the thing, though. How could you ever prove if they'd used a synthetic voice or not?

MEL. You couldn't.

ROD. Even if they reach this agreement.

MEL. Sooner or later we will all be fucked, won't we?

The shower goes off.

ROD. I got that telly I went for, by the way.

MEL. Did you? Well done.

ROD. One year with an option.

MEL. You must be thrilled.

ROD *comes out of the bathroom in jeans, drying himself.*

ROD. I don't know, though. Memphis isn't sure a soap's the right thing for me at the moment.

MEL. It's a soap, is it?

ROD. Yeah, *EastEnders*. (*He starts ironing.*)

MEL. It's *EastEnders*.

ROD. Crap part, though. Whoever remembers the vicar in *EastEnders*? I think I'm gonna turn it down.

MEL. Are you . . . ? Can I ask you a favour, then?

ROD. Sure.

MEL. D'you mind not saying anything to the others about it?

ROD. No, why?

MEL. Because . . . Greg went up for that part.

ROD. You're joking. He's far too old.

MEL. Yeah, well, please don't say anything for now.

ROD. Sure. Nuff said.

MEL. Thanks.

ROD. I mean, if I could just get this movie. I'm meeting the producer. Memphis thinks they want a newcomer. How do you think I should play it?

MEL. Memphis?

ROD. Yeah. Paddy's agent, Memphis Ball. He's taken me on.

MEL. Oh, has he?

ROD. Yeah. It's all honeymoony at the moment.

MEL. I'm sure.

ROD. He's great, isn't he, Paddy? So how do you think I should play it? With this producer?

MEL. Oh, well, I'd be rather cool about it.

ROD (*putting on his shirt*). Do you like this shirt?

MEL. Yes.

ROD. Do you think it suits me?

MEL. Yes, it does.

ROD. Really?

MEL. Yes.

ROD. Thanks. How come you're still here?

MEL shrugs.

Do you fancy a drink?

MEL. What about your meeting?

ROD. No, I mean after. I think you need a bit of cheering up. After a headfull of that shit. Would you like to go dancing?

MEL. Pardon?

ROD. Go on. I know a great little club. But it's not clubby.

MEL. Er . . . I don't know.

ROD. I won't be long . . .

MEL. I suppose I could wait.

ROD. Go on.

MEL. All right then.

ROD. I think you're awesome.

He kisses her.

Blackout.

Five

NEWS REPORTER (*voice-over*). At the forefront of the union's campaign have been some of the real heavyweights of the profession. None more so than Digby Scott, here seen on the picket line in Soho Square. Remembered perhaps by some of our older viewers, and leading very much by example.

DIGBY (*voice-over*). Of course, a long protracted strike could be very damaging for our industry. I'm just hoping some sense will be seen by all. Thank you.

Six

The music for the anagram puzzle on the Channel Four series Countdown *is playing. It comes to an end. Lights up on the flat. Late afternoon.* GREG, MEL *and* PADDY *are all watching the TV and doing the anagram.*

MEL. Seven. 'Creator'.

GREG. Three. 'Car'.

PADDY. Eight letters. 'Cavorted'.

> DIGBY *enters in his donkey jacket.* PADDY *turns the TV off.*

DIGBY. God, it was fantastic out there. I haven't felt so vital in years. The studios don't know what's hit them. And because everyone was so fantastically on their voices we managed to make a right old racket. And Pig got hold of that arsehole presenter and thumped him.

MEL. Which arsehole presenter?

GREG. He did what?

DIGBY. That poncy-car bloke.

MEL. What poncy-car bloke?

DIGBY. Oh, you'd know him. Never off the fucking box.

MEL. What, Jeremy Clarkson?

DIGBY. That's the one. Caught him sneaking out of the building. Pig got the bastard up against the wall and had it out with him.

GREG. He hit Jeremy Clarkson?

DIGBY. The worm had just done a telly ad, and Pig sniffed him out.

PADDY. Pig hit Jeremy Clarkson?

DIGBY. A belter. Cameras were there and everything. Hasn't he got a huge head?

MEL. Oh no.

DIGBY. Said the strike was nothing to do with him. Poor old Pig was led away.

PADDY. Pig was led away!

DIGBY. A martyr to the cause.

PADDY. A martyr to the cause!

DIGBY. Are you going to repeat everything I say?

PADDY. Digby, I'm shocked.

MEL. Was Rod down there?

DIGBY. Oh, Rod's been marvellous. He's been doing the Starbuck run.

GREG. That's lucky, then.

The phone rings.

DIGBY. I had to slope off after the fracas unfortunately. I've agreed to do a charity appeal. But I think we're making a real impression. And this early evening shift is tremendously important.

TOM (*on answerphone*). Mel, it's me. Two things. Firstly, I had a long chat with the solicitor, which you're paying for by the way, and even if you give up work altogether it's not going to make any difference because –

DIGBY *picks up the phone.*

DIGBY. Oh, fuck off.

He puts the phone down.

MEL. Thank you.

DIGBY. And what about you? Any news?

GREG. I didn't get it. I just didn't get it. OK? And I don't want to talk about it. I've moved on.

DIGBY. Fuck 'em.

GREG. Yeah.

DIGBY. You wouldn't know who played this by any chance, would you? (*He sings a few bars of 'Pasadena' by the Temperance Seven*) What were they called? Come on. They were the Seven . . . It was a bit before your time, I know. But it is a very well known piece. Jazz. Trumpet has the tune. It was the Seven . . . Seven . . . (*Hums the tune again with eyes closed.*) It was Blackheath. '73. At the summer fair. I was pissed as a plum. And mad about a gypsy called Ivan. God, he was something. Dark, dark hair and olive skin. He ran the donkey rides at the fair on Blackheath. It was the Something Seven. Christ. Why can't I remember it? He played it all the time. I wanted to run away with him. He had one of those caravans. Temperance Seven. Got it. I'm changing record number three to Pasadena. (*Sings a few lines.*) The Temperance Seven. '73. Blackheath. Right. All set?

PADDY. Talking of donkeys, Digby, where exactly did you find all these jackets?

DIGBY. Wardrobe store at the National.

The phone rings. As they leave, DIGBY *starts handing out the placards.*

We've got a job lot. A production of *King Lear*, apparently. Christ knows what they were doing in donkey jackets, but it's working a treat in West One. Come on.

TOM (*on answerphone*). Mel, it's Tom. I didn't find that particularly amusing. However, the second thing I had to tell you was –

The door slams shut.

Blackout.

Seven

NEWS REPORTER (*voice-over*). Terence Piggott-Jones, seen here leaving Charing Cross Police Station this afternoon, has been bailed to appear before Bow Street Magistrates'

Court following his recent arrest during the disturbances in Soho Square. It marks a rather sour end to the strike, after their union struck a three-year deal regulating the use of digitally-enhanced voices in the industry. Insiders have been quick to point out –

Later on. PADDY *and* GREG *enter. They carry a case of champagne each.* MEL *enters a few moments later, also carrying a case of champagne. She is followed by* DIGBY, *who is feverish. He sits.*

DIGBY. I couldn't quite manage it, I'm afraid.

PADDY. I'll go.

DIGBY. Not there. Mind the CDs.

MEL. How are you feeling?

DIGBY. Yes. Fine. Just caught a bit of a chill, that's all.

MEL. Why is it when I get paid in kind it's Christmas cards or wicker baskets?

PADDY *comes back in with the other case and starts to open it.*

DIGBY. You're obviously appealing to the wrong charities.

PADDY. It's good stuff, this. Not cheap.

MEL. Actually, I was given 'his and hers' watches once, but they had 'Sunny Farm Prunes' written all over them.

PADDY. Charming.

MEL. They kept very good time, though. I gave them to the kids.

PADDY. Four bloody cases, though! What did you have to do for four cases?

DIGBY. It was a very tricky read.

MEL. 'A very tricky read'!

DIGBY. It was at least a minute masquerading as a thirty-second body.

MEL. What charity was it?

DIGBY. Something awareness or other. Now look, you've got to move on, Greg. It was only a soap.

MEL. But to keep him hanging on like that.

DIGBY. Par for the course these days.

MEL. There'll be something better round the corner.

PADDY. It was obviously not meant to be.

GREG. Can we just . . . leave it. It went the other way. So can we please . . . move on.

DIGBY. Why don't we open a couple of bottles? I think the sun's over the yardarm.

PADDY. I'll get some glasses.

DIGBY. Come on, Greg.

GREG. I really thought this time I had it. My name was written all over it.

DIGBY. And chill a few more in the freezer, would you? In fact, I'm feeling generous. I want to give you each a case.

MEL. Digby!

PADDY. Thank you, Digby.

MEL. What a lovely surprise.

DIGBY. It's been a long haul, after all.

GREG. On the barricades.

DIGBY. And I think you've all done very well. I've actually been very proud. So thank you. Even Paddy.

PADDY. Thank you, sir.

DIGBY. And we mustn't be despondent. A three-year agreement is better than no agreement.

PADDY. Hear, hear.

DIGBY. So here's to us.

MEL. The flying pickets.

DIGBY. Cheers, everyone, and well done.

PADDY. Yes.

MEL. Cheers.

PADDY. Up the workers.

DIGBY. And there was something else that I –

MEL. Oh, that is lovely.

PADDY. Mmmm. That is V good.

DIGBY. That I wanted to –

MEL. That is lovely.

PADDY. Very moreish.

DIGBY. – that I wanted to ask you all.

PADDY. There's something I have to say as well.

MEL. I have to admit I was never comfortable with the chanting.

DIGBY. What do you mean?

MEL. Shouting out things like 'I know where you live'.

DIGBY. Well, I did know where the bastard lived.

MEL. I don't care. You shouldn't have done it.

DIGBY. Right. Well, anyway, that wasn't what I wanted to say. Firstly, I want to thank you all for your patience over the last few weeks with regard to my *Desert Island Discs*. It hasn't been easy choosing which pieces of music to take . . . to accompany those important moments in my life, but I feel when I'm sitting in that chair, I can genuinely say . . . this has been one of the most important times in my life. The flat and all of you.

ALL (*variously*). The flat. / To us all. / Hear, hear.

PADDY. Digby. The *Desert Island Discs* –

DIGBY. Please, Paddy, no more interruptions. And secondly, I wanted to ask you – and the timely arrival of the champagne was entirely appropriate – because I was wondering how we'd all feel if I asked Rod to come on board with the flat. (*Beat.*) We haven't had any fresh blood for years. It's long overdue, and I think Rod's got just the right balance of what we could all do with around here.

PADDY. And what's that?

GREG. A big brown nose and a nice arse to stick it right up. Digby! Get a grip. The boy's a chancer. He's using you.

DIGBY. And of course you never did.

GREG. He's wormed his way in here. Snapped up Sharon, leeched himself onto Memphis –

DIGBY. He needed a helping hand. As you did. That doesn't make him a terrible person. Mel, you like him, don't you?

GREG. Wait a minute.

MEL. Yes. I like him, but –

DIGBY. Good.

GREG. I know why you like him.

MEL. Oh, really?

GREG. You've been plotting this, haven't you?

DIGBY. Paddy?

PADDY. Well I . . . I think he's –

MEL. No one's been plotting anything.

PADDY. I don't know. He's er . . . He's –

GREG. Seen you as Hotspur in *Henry IV* and probably wants to suck your cock as well –

MEL. Greg, stop.

DIGBY. I won't have this in –

GREG. In what? Your flat? We share this flat, Digby.

PADDY. Look, I –

GREG. Paddy, why aren't you with me on this one?

DIGBY. He's vibrant, and enthusiastic –

GREG. And a wonderful masseur –

DIGBY. You're jealous.

GREG. No, I'm not.

DIGBY. It's the young stag.

GREG. The what?

DIGBY (*loudly*). The young stag.

GREG. I heard you. As opposed to the young shag, you mean? You hardly know him.

PADDY. He'd be paying his share of the rent, wouldn't he?

GREG. Working for you, no doubt.

PADDY. What's that supposed to mean?

MEL. Anyway, Greg. I'd like to go away and think about it –

GREG. I thought he was a bit of a natural, Mel, didn't you?

MEL. We should all have a proper think.

DIGBY. What are you talking about?

MEL. Digby. It is a big thing, someone else coming in on the flat –

GREG. Shall I tell him?

DIGBY. What did he mean by that? Working for Paddy?

PADDY. I don't think that would be entirely appropriate. Do you, old fruit?

DIGBY. Paddy?

GREG. Paddy's got a little sideline, haven't you?

MEL. Greg!

GREG. He's got a dodgy little business dubbing porn films.

MEL. Oh God.

GREG. We all work for him now and again. But he didn't want you knowing about it. I think he's a bit embarrassed, to tell you the truth. Well, we all are really, aren't we, 'gang'? But when you've done it once, it doesn't seem so bad the next time. Then before you know it you're working with animals and all sorts. He's even got your bright young star on board.

DIGBY. Rod?

GREG. Yup.

DIGBY. He's got Rod . . .

GREG. 'Fraid so.

PADDY. No one forced him to do it. No one forced any of you.

GREG. And – get this, Digby – he's not even paying the boy the union rate.

MEL. Why are you doing this?

PADDY. I was doing him a favour.

GREG. I must say, he was terribly good, dubbing all that fucking. What do you think, Mel?

MEL. I think you should shut up. What was the point of that? Are you happy now?

GREG. Yeah. I am. I'm starting to feel better already.

PADDY. Really? You can hear me then, can you? Loud and clear? Because that'll make a change.

GREG. What?

PADDY. Ah, not quite so good, then. Or is it selective hearing you're best at?

GREG (to MEL). All right then, shall we tell them?

DIGBY. What the hell is this?

GREG. I've got tinnitus.

DIGBY. What?

GREG. I've got tinnitus, Digby. It means I get a ringing in my ears all the time. It means –

DIGBY. I know what it means.

GREG. And there's nothing I can do. There isn't any medication or any treatment. I just have to learn to live with it. Or go mad. That's why I'm screwing up sessions and losing work.

A key turns in the door and ROD *enters.*

ROD. Hi. I've come around the right time, haven't I? I hope it's OK – I used the keys you gave me.

MEL. Champagne?

ROD. Yes please.

DIGBY. I didn't know you'd been working for Paddy.

ROD. What?

DIGBY. I hear you've been working for Paddy.

ROD. I was told not to tell you.

DIGBY. Oh, really?

ROD. They said you wouldn't approve.

DIGBY. If it was money you needed, you only had to ask.

MEL. It's not that bad, Digby.

DIGBY. Oh yes it is.

PADDY. And Mr Sheen is class, is it?

ROD. I think I better come back another time. You've obviously got some issues you need to work through.

DIGBY. The only 'issue' that needs 'working through' is the one concerning my invitation to you to join our fucked-up little colony on the Soho sea. And Greg's objection to it.

ROD. What's your objection?

DIGBY. He doubts your integrity.

ROD. He doubts my integrity? Why? What is it I've done?

DIGBY. I don't think it's anything you've done, Rod. I think it's Greg who has the problem.

MEL. Do we have to have this now?

ROD. I didn't mean to cause any friction. I'm sorry. The last thing I wanted was to tread on any toes. I just thought you all –

GREG. I think you're a bit of a chancer. Muscling in here.

ROD. 'Muscling in'! Oh, forget it. Forget the whole thing.

DIGBY. Rod!

   ROD *stops at the door.*

ROD (*to* GREG). I mean, you talk about my integrity – calling me a chancer! What about you? You're saying one thing and doing another.

MEL. Rod! Wait a minute, there's no need –

ROD. Why haven't you got the bottle to stand up for what you think is right? If you do think it's right.

DIGBY. If you think what's right?

MEL. Rod –

ROD. One minute he's recording a TV commercial, the next minute he's standing on the picket line.

DIGBY. What?

GREG. Don't look at me like that. The strike was bollocks –

DIGBY. Christ! You've been standing with me on a picket line!

GREG. To keep you happy.

DIGBY. To keep me happy!

GREG. Yes! I didn't want to rock the boat.

DIGBY. You didn't want to rock the boat? I think the boat's well and truly sunk, don't you?

GREG. It's technology, Digby. No one can stop it. They'll find a way to use man-made voices.

DIGBY. You unprincipled shit!

GREG. The union has no power any more. We've moved on.

DIGBY. Well, the things that I'm talking about don't 'move on'.

GREG. So you want to drag as many of us down with you as you can?

DIGBY. I'm sorry, I won't –

GREG. It could be ball bearings, Digby. What we're doing. No one cares any more. You're out of touch.

DIGBY. I beg your pardon?

GREG. You're out of touch –

DIGBY. I heard you –

GREG. It's about being practical, Digby. Common sense. We've got to work with these people, while we can. It's pointless not doing it.

DIGBY. Get out.

GREG. This is about money.

DIGBY. No, it's not about the money.

GREG. Yes it is. That's all it's about.

DIGBY. Fuck the money! It's about principle, Greg.

GREG. You hypocritical bastard! After the pile you've made.

DIGBY. It's about respect and integrity and whether our profession lives or dies.

GREG. Wake up, Digby! Everyone's been breaking the fucking strike. No one cares.

ROD. Well, Digby cares, and so do I.

GREG. Oh, fuck off!

DIGBY attacks GREG. ROD looks on as MEL and PADDY pull them apart.

MEL. Jesus Christ.

Silence. ROD goes.

DIGBY. Porn empire. I don't know how you find the time to fit it all in. I suppose it's all a bit of a joke to you, isn't it? Like everything else in your sad, suburban life –

PADDY. Here we go. Come on. Let's hear it, then. About my pathetic little life.

DIGBY. Just a bit of a laugh. So you don't have to care too much.

PADDY. All you need now's your crown of thorns.

DIGBY. In case anyone finds out just how vacuous you really are. (*To* MEL.) And you? I'm very disappointed. Why didn't you tell me any of this?

MEL. Because I didn't think it was my business to tell you other people's secrets, Digby. I don't tell anyone yours.

DIGBY. Oh, go away, all of you. Don't speak to me. (*Beat.*) I'll have to change the whole of the last section now. Record number eight. Everything. You've screwed up the whole shape.

PADDY. Oh, for goodness' sake, Digby. There's no *Desert Island Discs*.

DIGBY. What?

PADDY. I said there isn't any *Desert Island Discs*. It was a joke.

DIGBY. What are you talking about?

MEL. Oh God, Paddy. What have you done?

PADDY. I just . . . It was meant to be a joke. A wind-up. It was supposed to be . . . (*Puts on a voice.*) 'Hello, Mr Scott, it's Jock from the *Desert Island Discs* production office.' (*Beat.*) I was going to tell him. I've been trying to tell you. I'm sorry. I thought you'd twig. You'd recognise my voice and laugh, or tell me to fuck off. You see, there he was, slagging me off all the time so I . . . I'm sorry, Digby.

DIGBY. If you'll excuse me.

DIGBY *leaves*.

MEL. How could you do that? How could you be so cruel?

PADDY. What about you? You fucked his lover boy. Or doesn't that count?

MEL *looks at* PADDY.

He told me.

MEL. Ah. Did he?

PADDY. Yes, he said he thought you needed cheering up.

MEL. It didn't mean anything.

PADDY. So it doesn't count, then?

PADDY *goes.* MEL *sits. She looks at the answerphone and sees that there is a message. She plays it.*

TOM (*on answerphone*). Mel, it's Tom. I didn't find that particularly amusing. However, the second thing I had to tell you was that Charlie broke his wrist falling off the monkey bars today. He's been asking for you. I've tried the mobile, but you're switched off as usual. If you get this and it's still a reasonable hour can you come and see him or give him a call? Bye.

Blackout.

Eight

DIGBY *is in a sound studio listening to his own voice-over. The other people we only hear.*

DIGBY (*voice-over*). 'In 1962, London Bridge was falling down into the clay of Old Father Thames, and folks laughed when a chainsaw magnate announced he'd bought it for

over two million dollars. Well . . . they stopped laughing
when it arrived in the Arizona desert. Stone by stone it was
reconstructed and pretty soon the town of Lake Havasu was
fat with cash. So now you can enjoy double scoops from
our double-decker, or explore the one-acre Olde London
Village at the foot of the historic bridge. 'Cause just
remember . . . old bridges never die, they retire to Lake
Havasu City.'

HANK. Hank here, Mr Scott. That was pretty much how I heard
it in my head. So if you could pretty much keep it there.
We'll be seeing shots of the bridge, the double-decker and
ye olde village. So on the next pass, could you just take
your time and give me a whole bigger bunch of that English
stuff.

MARVIN (*sound engineer*). Hold it, Hank. I just need to check
the level. Could you give us a couple of lines, sir? If you
could just give us a couple of lines, please, for a level?

DIGBY. A level. Right. (*Beat.*)
'To sleep, perchance to dream. Ay there's the rub;
For in that sleep of – '

MARVIN. Thank you, sir, that's great. We'll go on the cue
light –

DIGBY.
'For in that sleep of death what dreams may come?
When we have shuffled off this mortal coil,
Must give us pause – '

HANK. Wow, that really is something, Mr Scott. I have a mind
we could use some of that. What is that from, sir?

DIGBY. I beg your pardon?

HANK. That recitation, sir. What is that from and do we have
a rights issue?

DIGBY. What?

HANK. I'm just wondering if we'd have to outlay to acquire
the rights.

DIGBY. It's from *Hamlet*.

HANK. I see. *Hamlet*. (*To* MARVIN.) Can you write that down? Anyways, Mr Scott. Let's roll up them sleeves and sell some double scoops. On the green, thank you.

DIGBY. 'In 1962, London Bridge was falling down into the clay of Old Father Thames . . . and folks laughed when . . . laughed when . . . '

DIGBY *breaks down*.

HANK. That was nice. (*Beat*.) Mr Scott?

DIGBY *starts humming, then singing to himself*.

What is that? Is that – ? Is he – ? Are you singing, sir?

DIGBY. I have a lot of memories from 1962. A lot of memories indeed. On the Isle of Wight. (*Sings 'You were made for me'*.) My first kiss under the pier at Shanklin. Oh, my first kiss. My first kiss from a man, that is –

HANK. Sir, may I remind you, you have a script and –

DIGBY. Don't look too hard into the light. Or he'll disappear –

HANK. Is he – ? Sir, are you – ?

DIGBY. He was so beautiful he took my breath away. Not quite a man, but not still a boy. We danced and laughed and held each other's hand. No one saw us. It was our secret place, in the dark. I was always first to hide and he would always find me. Such ghosts. The shadows of our paths not taken.

DIGBY *collapses*.

Blackout.

Nine

Six weeks later. In the flat. GREG *has a device on his ear like a hearing aid. He is looking at the instructions and fiddling with it.* PADDY *is watching TV.* MEL *is packing some slippers for* DIGBY.

MEL. What do you think? These are all right, aren't they?

PADDY. Yeah. They're nice.

MEL. Choice was rather limited.

PADDY. He'll like those.

MEL. I'm taking them in this evening. The ones he's got are so threadbare.

GREG. What?

MEL. I'm taking these in to the hospital.

GREG. He can't wear them, though, can he?

MEL. No, but he'll have them.

PADDY. Are his feet really that small?

GREG. Do you want me to come with you?

MEL. It's easier for him if we go separately.

GREG. I think it's easier for him if we go separately.

MEL. Good. I'll tell him. You will go?

GREG. Yes. I said I'll go tomorrow. I've not exactly got much on.

PADDY (*referring to the TV*). Oh look, there's our lovely boy. (*He turns the sound up again.*)

ROD (*voice-over*).'Where there was darkness there will be light. Where there was misunderstanding there will be knowledge. Where there is chaos let there be Gonnadoo.'

PADDY (*switching sound off*). They're playing it all the time.

GREG. Fucking arsehole.

MEL. The ward sister asked if I was his daughter today. (*Beat.*) There really isn't anyone else, you know.

PADDY. Could you remind him that I'm coming on Friday afternoon? I told him yesterday, but I'm don't know if he took it in.

MEL. OK.

GREG. I thought he had a brother in the Mumbles.

MEL. They're not in touch. What about the weekend? I can't this time because it's my weekend with the kids.

GREG. I'll go.

PADDY. Any more news on that front? Are you going to call his bluff?

MEL. I can't do it. I can't do it to them, Paddy. If I stop working they'll lose their home. And he'd probably still get custody anyway.

PADDY. Sorry. Oh, by the way, Memphis told me our lovely boy's going out to Hollywood.

GREG. What?

PADDY. He's got some enormous movie out there.

GREG. You're joking! How?

PADDY. American agent, everything. He's the new thing, apparently.

GREG. Is he?

MEL. I saw him last week.

GREG. You did what?

MEL. In Old Compton Street. He pretended not to see me. He was wearing a floor-length black leather coat.

GREG. Wanker!

MEL. He kept checking himself in the shop windows.

GREG. Arsehole!

MEL. Digby keeps asking if he's been in touch. It's awful.

GREG. He's never going to get in touch. Tosser! Who wears a floor-length black leather coat?

PADDY. Well, yours isn't too far off the knee.

GREG. I think it's despicable. He knows he's in intensive care with bloody pneumonia.

MEL. I don't know what to say to him.

GREG. Ah! Will you fuck this thing! These instructions are useless.

He takes the device off his ear and screws up the instructions.

It's useless. Worse than useless. Worse than the ringing. I'll see you all tomorrow.

GREG *leaves.*

PADDY (*voice-over*). 'Tony Mole recently received five thousand pounds for a work-related accident. Dawn Gates received eleven thousand pounds for breaking a bone on a loose paving slab – '

PADDY *mutes the TV.*

PADDY. Anyway, I've bought us a proper shower mat. Have you seen it?

MEL. Yes. He's so frail.

PADDY. Right, now if I'm focused and organised, I'll get that train. So I'll have to love you and leave you. And don't forget to remind him about Friday, will you?

MEL. I won't. Bye.

MEL *knocks back her glass of wine, turns off the TV and gets her coat. She picks up her bag and goes.*

The phone rings once. It's DIGBY. *His voice is changed, frail.*

DIGBY (*on answerphone*). Only me. I was hoping to catch you. Nothing urgent. Just wanted to know if you were coming in tonight. Oh, and er . . . just wondered if there's been any mail. A card or anything. One of those e-mails? I've been thinking . . . perhaps I should get a mobile phone or maybe I should get one of those blueberries. They do look rather swish. And I could get text messages then, couldn't I? What do you think? Anyway, hope all's well and, er . . . see you later, I expect.

End.